Discover your personal *Clarity Quotient* and accelerate your results now

Here's how you can start accelerating your results now: Discover your personal *Clarity Quotient* by answering 20 simple questions (multiple-choice). This quick and easy questionnaire gives you a snapshot of your current state of mind, including a stress score and an engagement score. You can get yours for free at

www.JamieSmart.com/CQ

T0339299

'*The Little Book of Results* provide a refreshing approach to personal and entrepreneurial transformation, and most importantly – to achieving results!'

Vlatka Hlupic, award-winning author of *The Management Shift*

'We all know we can have our best ideas, have a clarity of insight, at unexpected times. In this book, Jamie Smart shows how we can have more moments of lucid clarity and how we can marry that clarity with a propensity to action to achieve results.'

Peter Lake, Managing Director, Aztec Aspire

'Jamie Smart's book connects the dots . . . so often missing . . . between understanding and excellent, creative actions that get results in the real world. A very stimulating book!'

Steve Chandler, author of *Time Warrior*

'If you want to know what it really takes to get results and live your life to the fullest, this book is the answer. The human pursuit of success is never the problem. It's our understanding of how life works that gets in the way of our natural capacity to create, thrive and prosper as individuals and as a society. In a clear, engaging and practical way, Jamie lays out a crucial road map that will show you how getting results is far easier than you realize. Highly recommended.'

Chantal Burns, No. 1 bestselling author of *Instant Motivation*, www.consciousleadershipschool.com

'*The Little Book of Results: a quick guide to achieving big goals* is total wisdom power. Understanding what Jamie Smart presents will allow you the insights and realizations that awaken your innate ability to create truly transformative results.'

Mark Howard, PhD, Three Principles Institute

'*The Little Book of Results: a quick guide to achieving big goals* points you to the blueprint of where success truly comes from. This book will guide you to the source of lifechanging insights. Well-done Jamie!'

Catherine Casey, M.A. Clinical Psychology,
Principle Based Consultant

'*The Little Book of Results* is an insightful and impactful book that flies in the face of the all too common shallow and ineffective self-help advice. This book has the potential to make a significant positive impact on your life.'

Simon Hazeldine, bestselling author of *Neuro-Sell*

'In this compelling book, Jamie Smart de-mystifies what underlies true transformation and your ability to get results in any aspect of your personal and professional life. Put on your seat belt and be prepared to have your conventional way of seeing the world be rocked, while simultaneously being introduced to an exciting new way of perceiving yourself and your world!'

Dicken Bettinger, Ed.D., retired psychologist, global seminar
leader, founder of 3 Principles Mentoring,
and co-author of *Coming Home*

'The power of a clear mind is pretty much universally understood when it comes to stillness, tranquility, and happiness. Yet almost never is it linked to achievement, excellence, and consistent results. Until now. In this profound book, Jamie Smart walks us through the extraordinary (and innate) process of experiencing a shift of consciousness or change of heart, first. Then cultivating the outcomes of our dreams becomes as simple as one, two, three.'

Garret Kramer, founder of Inner Sports and author of
Stillpower and *The Path of No Resistance*

'The simple, yet profound, principles discussed in this book reveal our true nature and with it the inherent, natural potential to relax, enjoy life, be our authentic self, find clarity and create the results we want in our personal and professional lives.'

Rita Shuford, PhD

'It's perfect for those seeking to live out their purpose, looking for motivation and inspiration and those who want to challenge themselves and better understand the interconnectedness of personal and business transformation. This book is an incredible resource allowing you to have the clarity to be the change you want to see in the world!'

Conor Houston, Programme Director, Centre for Democracy and Peace Building

'This book is an insightful, powerful and unforgettable gem. Jamie Smart gently guides the reader to experience profound insights which will forever alter their view of reality – and transform their results. A must read!'

Carl Harvey, Founder, Abundance Book Club

'Simply captivating. Well articulated and to the point. *The Little Book of Results* is without a doubt Jamie's finest work yet. A must read for any busy business owner who wants to accelerate their results with less effort.'

Dan Bradbury, Entrepreneur and author of *Breeding Gazelles*

'*The Little Book of Results* is the blueprint for a world of more love, connection and true prosperity. We often live under the misunderstanding that motivation and success should come easy, when actually it takes courage. If you are willing to take that step, this is your book.'

Virginia Salas Kastilio, Snapchat Influencer, Speaker and Strategist; CEO of Gini.TV

'I have worked with the CLARITY principles personally and with my leadership team. The results we have achieved are remarkable in terms of the impact across our business, the velocity we are able to achieve these in and the engagement of our people into the leadership direction and vision. Clarity is our guiding principle as a team. Smart's new book *The Little Book of Results: a quick guide to achieving big goals* shows in a clear, easy-to-understand way what we've discovered through our own experience: that clarity plus action equals results!'

Murray Pearce, Managing Director, Infinigate UK

THE
LITTLE BOOK
OF
RESULTS

THE
LITTLE BOOK
OF

RESULTS

a quick guide to achieving
big goals

Jamie Smart

This edition first published 2018
© 2018 Jamie Smart
CLARITY® is a registered trademark of Jamie Smart Limited

Jamie Smart
John Wiley & Sons Ltd, The Atrium, Southern Gate, Chichester, West Sussex, PO19
8SQ, United Kingdom

For details of our global editorial offices, for customer services and for information
about how to apply for permission to reuse the copyright material in this book please
see our website at www.wiley.com.

Wiley publishes in a variety of print and electronic formats and by print-on-demand.
Some material included with standard print versions of this book may not be included in
e-books or in print-on-demand. If this book refers to media such as a CD or DVD that
is not included in the version you purchased, you may download this material at http://
booksupport.wiley.com. For more information about Wiley products, visit www.wiley.com.

Designations used by companies to distinguish their products are often claimed as
trademarks. All brand names and product names used in this book are trade names,
service marks, trademarks or registered trademarks of their respective owners. The
publisher is not associated with any product or vendor mentioned in this book.

Limit of Liability/Disclaimer of Warranty: While the publisher and author have used
their best efforts in preparing this book, they make no representations or warranties
with respect to the accuracy or completeness of the contents of this book and
specifically disclaim any implied warranties of merchantability or fitness for a particular
purpose. It is sold on the understanding that the publisher is not engaged in rendering
professional services and neither the publisher nor the author shall be liable for damages
arising herefrom. If professional advice or other expert assistance is required, the services
of a competent professional should be sought.

Library of Congress Cataloging-in-Publication Data is Available

ISBN 978-0-857-08780-5 (paperback)
ISBN 978-0-857-08771-3 (ePub)
ISBN 978-0-857-08781-2 (ePDF)

Cover design: Wiley

Set in 10/13pts Sabon by SPi Global, Chennai, India
Printed in Great Britain by TJ International Ltd, Padstow, Cornwall, UK

10 9 8 7 6 5 4 3 2 1

To all the people around the world who have caught a glimpse of the principles behind clarity and are pointing others in this direction

Contents

Preface

....

After *The Little Book of Clarity* was released in 2015, I lost count of the number of people who told me how much they'd enjoyed the book, then confided that they thought it was actually *better* than its big brother, *CLARITY*. My response to these congratulations was strangely polarized; on the one hand, I felt delighted they'd enjoyed the new book. And on the other hand, I felt protective of its predecessor. I anticipate there will be more of this to come with the release of *The Little Book of Results*.

When my book *RESULTS: Think Less, Achieve More* was launched in 2016, it received an excellent response, becoming a Sunday Times bestseller almost immediately. I knew it would make sense to write the concise version, but I also knew it would require me to brutally edit the original book, so I made a decision: I would remove everything except those elements which were utterly crucial to conveying the book's central message. The task was often challenging and sometimes painful, but the results will, I hope, speak for themselves.

So why a *Little Book of Results*?

RESULTS addressed the challenge of how to thrive, have an impact and do the things that matter to you in a rapidly changing world. We live in times of increasing volatility, uncertainty, complexity and ambiguity. In the 18 months since *RESULTS* was written, the world has continued to transform in ways that are often surprising and sometimes dramatic (facilitated in large part by the acceleration of digital technology).

In *RESULTS*, I referenced a report (*Future Work Skills 2020*) created by *The Institute for the Future* (IFTF) describing the skills workers are going to need in response to the trends sweeping our world. The capabilities range from social intelligence and cross-cultural competency to new media literacy and cognitive load management. Then, as I was writing *The Little Book of Results*, the IFTF released an update to their report explaining that they'd overlooked an essential competency; *resilience*. Your innate capacity for resilience is just one of the deep drivers you're going to be 'igniting' as you read this book, and it is essential if you're going to navigate the challenges—and capitalise on the opportunities—that the future holds.

The message at the heart of this book is more urgent and important than ever. You're capable of more than you think because you *are* more than you think. We are all born results-creators. The purpose of this book is to help you fully realise that birthright so you can live the life you desire and create the results that matter to you and for you.

To your increasing clarity and results!
Jamie Smart, 2018

THE
LITTLE BOOK
OF
RESULTS

Introduction

....

However beautiful the strategy, you should occasionally look at the results.

Sir Winston Churchill, Former UK Prime Minister, winner of the Nobel Prize in Literature, 1953

'What's the number one result that you believe would have the biggest positive impact in your life?'

Over the years, I've asked variations on this 'number one result' question to many thousands of people during talks, workshops and one-to-one coaching sessions. And while their backgrounds are incredibly diverse, their initial response is remarkably similar. Invariably, people. . .

Stop. . . Go quiet. . . Get reflective. . .

Your biggest return on investment

As the responses begin to emerge, they reveal something very powerful. Your answer to this question shows what you currently *believe* would give you your biggest 'return on investment' (ROI) for the time, energy, effort and other resources it would take to achieve it. When I was first asked the question by my coach (a successful entrepreneur) in 2006, I didn't know the answer, and I felt foolish. After all, I *should* know, shouldn't I? I was working 14-hour days growing my business, but if I didn't know the answer to this, what was I spending all my time, energy and money on? This powerful, unsettling question issued a challenge:

> *Are you willing to raise your head from the daily routine of tasks, habits and distractions, and focus your energy on what matters most to you, no matter how daunting that may seem? Are you willing to shift your attention from the soothing familiarity of 'routine' to the sometimes-uncomfortable adventure of 'results'?*

Results. . .

We all want them, yet many of us struggle to achieve them. Or we get spectacular results in *one* area of life, while failing to attain even modest success in other important areas. There are plenty of examples. . .

- The successful businessman who knows he needs to lose weight and get fit, but never seems to find the time.

- The manager who's passionate about becoming a consultant or executive coach, but fears stepping away from the security of a full-time job.

- The graduate who wants to find work with meaning and purpose, but doesn't know where to start.

- The therapist who has a big impact on her clients, but struggles to make ends meet.

- The CEO who wants to leapfrog the competition, but can't find the right strategy.

You probably know someone who dreams of writing the book/ starting the business/clearing the debts/finding the soulmate/ creating the lifestyle/getting the six-pack/making that first million, but never quite seems to get there. You may even *be* that person.

Five essential questions

Motivational speakers claim we can achieve whatever we want if we believe in ourselves, set clear goals and work hard. But history is littered with examples where enormous self-belief combined with clear goals and massive action yielded *few or no* satisfying results. Why? As you're going to discover, there are powerful but little-known factors that have a profound impact on your ability to create results. In fact, this book sets out to answer five essential questions:

1 What are the key factors that influence your ability to create the results you desire, and how can you develop those factors?

2 What are the obstacles that may have been holding you or your organization back from getting the results you want, and how can you avoid, eliminate or overcome those obstacles?

3 How can you increase your impact on other people, engaging them in *your* enterprises and/or empowering them to create the results *they* desire?

4 How can you leverage your true nature as a results-creator and a leader to get greater control of your livelihood, whether as a solopreneur, as an entrepreneur or by playing a bigger role in your organization?

5 How can you do all of this in a way that's healthy, natural, authentic and enjoyable?

I've spent the past 17 years helping my clients to create results that are often beyond anything they'd previously thought possible. I've worked with. . .

- business leaders and their teams to create inspiring visions that they've proceeded to bring into existence

- coaches, therapists and other transformation professionals to increase their impact, grow their practices and create life-styles they love

- entrepreneurs to get clarity, transform their personal and professional lives and achieve breakthrough results

- private individuals ranging from maximum-security prison inmates to chart-topping DJs; from alcoholics and drug addicts to surgeons and opera singers.

The fact that they've done it means that you can do it too. The fact that you're even *reading* this means you have an innate capacity to live a life you love and create meaningful results in the process. And I don't want you to take my word for it. Instead, as you read this book, I'll be inviting you to test my claims in your own life and against your personal experience so you can discover the truth of this for yourself. It doesn't even matter if you don't yet know what results you want to create. As you deepen your understanding of the principles we'll be exploring together, you're going to start seeing your world with new eyes, getting clarity about what you want to bring into being, and having it happen in ways you may never have anticipated until now.

Your results may be closer than you think

The first time I was asked the *number one result* question, I eventually managed to identify the thing I believed would give me the most leverage. I wanted to generate income by putting my educational products online so I could stop selling my time, and put my energy into growing my business. 'How long do you think it will take to do that?' my coach asked. I told her I thought it would take between 18 months and 3 years. This was the same answer I'd come up with when I'd first had the idea, 18 months previously. In fact, that '18 months to 3 years' timeline always seemed to be floating ahead of me, keeping my goal the same elusive distance away, like a juicy carrot dangling from a pole attached to a donkey's head. But it turned out that my estimate was wrong by several orders of magnitude; in the end, it only took six weeks. As is so often the case, it turned out that I had a lot of the pieces in place, but hadn't realized it (it's very likely that this is the case for you too). In the process, I discovered one of the most important things you can learn about creating results:

There's a shortest possible time required for you to create a result, but nobody knows how long that shortest possible time is. The only way to discover it is experimentally, by taking action.

Your results may be closer than you think. Of course, we live in a material world, and there are certain universal laws or 'principles' that cannot be violated (e.g. the principle of gravity).

But all too often it is not material laws, but rather our *beliefs, concepts and misunderstandings* which place artificial limits on the results we produce, on the impact we have and on our enjoyment of life in general.

The process of transformation

By early 2008, my business was running on autopilot and I was ready to celebrate with my first 'mini-retirement', a three-month holiday at a Canadian ski resort. I was delighted with what my team and I had accomplished, and I believed this trip would yield another satisfying result; a big jump in my skiing ability combined with a sense of peace, completeness and success. But I was wrong. After a brief period of euphoria, I found myself distracted and dissatisfied, with a busy mind and feeling like there was something missing. I felt stuck, so I cut my trip short and flew home without realizing I was at the very beginning of a massive transformation; a transformation that would see me. . .

- sell the business I'd spent so much time and energy developing,

- walk away from the field I'd become a leader in, and

- start over, moving in an entirely new direction.

That was ten years ago, and they've been some of the most exciting, fulfilling, challenging and joyful years of my life. It's been (and continues to be) a process of transformation. And that, in essence, is the purpose of this book: to guide you in the process of more and more fully embracing your *true nature* as a results-creator. For reasons of clarity and simplicity, the process is organized around three distinct transformations:

Part One – GROUNDING
Your Personal Transformation

Imagine you're building a skyscraper; the higher you want the building to go, the deeper the foundation has to be. The purpose of Part One is to help you develop your foundations: the key qualities and internal resources of a powerful results-creator. While grounding is the foundation piece, it's often the last place people look when it comes to creating outstanding results. Your grounding is what governs your ability to move forward in the face of uncertainty, and make a real difference in the world. Grounding also determines the impact you're able to have on others, whether as a business leader, a coach, a parent, a partner or a friend. This is the deep understanding of yourself and the human condition that is the basis for all powerful transformation. You're going to be introduced to *subtractive psychology*, simple but powerful principles that will start clearing your mind and awakening your innate capacities. As you move through your personal transformation, you're going to find yourself experiencing certain *automatic and inevitable results*. You may notice that you're developing greater confidence, clarity and peace of mind. You're also likely to find yourself experiencing a reduction in stress, worry and anxiety. As you approach the end of Part One, you may start becoming aware of a greater sense of purpose, direction and leadership as you start taking action and moving forward.

Part Two – IMPACT
Your Interpersonal Transformation

As human beings, we have a more highly evolved capacity for connection and relationship than any other species on the planet. It's not only a highly effective survival strategy (it's made us the world's most deadly predators); it's also an extraordinary leverage point when it comes to creating results. The purpose of Part Two is to support you in creating connection and impact in *all* your relationships. Your interpersonal transformation will give you the confidence and ability to have a greater impact on others, secure in the knowledge that you have something of genuine value and relevance to contribute. Whether as a business leader, a transformation professional, a parent or a colleague, impact means the difference between making a difference and wasting your breath. You're going to be introduced to the *Clarity Impact Model*, the tried and tested tool used by some of the world's most impactful coaches, consultants and therapists. In this section you should start to notice certain results emerging easily as the result of your being exposed to the principles in this book. You're going to be discovering the kind of effortless relationship skills that are the essence of powerful communication, whether you're giving a presentation, selling a prospect, coaching a colleague or connecting with your loved ones. You're also going to discover the secrets to dealing with difficult people, and the unexpected keys for motivating others to make changes and take action.

Part Three – LEVERAGE
Your Commercial Transformation

Your commercial transformation is about amplifying your impact, taking control of your livelihood, and moving into a world of abundance through connection, innovation and service. Whether you're an employee in an organization, running your own business or are looking to transition from one to the other, a service-orientation combined with new-economy savvy are essential for taking control of your commercial transformation and creating the livelihood you desire. You're going to be transforming your relationship to prosperity, and taking charge of your income as you awaken your inner entrepreneur (whether as a solopreneur, business owner or a star player in a larger organization). You'll be learning how to move with the disruptive forces transforming the business world, and learning how to thrive in the increasing complexity of the commercial landscape.

Subtractive psychology: Less is more

While this book is divided into three sections for practical purposes, they actually describe three different aspects of *one* transformation: the process of becoming the person who can create the results you're here to create, and more fully live the life you're here to live. Most approaches for creating results are *additive*, giving you theories, techniques and concepts to remember, practise and apply. While additive approaches are often compelling, they rarely yield the desired results (for reasons we'll explore later). Fortunately, the understanding you're going to be developing as you read this book is *subtractive*. Instead of giving you more to remember, the principles you're going to be learning will take things off your mind, giving you *less* to think about. As a result, you're going to have a clear mind more of the time and more space for the endeavours and experiences that matter.

We are living in a VUCA world

We are in a time of increasing volatility, uncertainty, complexity and ambiguity (VUCA). Silicon Valley startups are disrupting entire industries. Airbnb was recently valued at $31 billion (March 2017), making it more valuable than the Hyatt Hotels Corporation or the InterContinental Hotels Group (owner of Holiday Inn and Crowne Plaza). This despite the fact that Airbnb has a fraction of the number of employees and owns *no hotels*. Uber, valued at $69 billion (July 2017), continues to dominate the taxi trade in many of the world's largest cities. Book-lovers are using bookshops as unofficial 'Amazon showrooms', browsing the books on display then ordering the ones they want on their smartphones or downloading them to their Kindles. While no-one knows what the future will bring to these companies and these industries, one thing is clear; the world is changing fast and it's unlikely to slow down anytime soon. These turbulent times bring both risk and opportunity. The purpose of this book is to help you mitigate the risks and make the most of the opportunities while enjoying your life to the full.

At the end of each chapter you'll find. . .

- **Bottom line results,** a concise summary highlighting how this chapter applies in the business/commercial context.

- A **Practicality check** to connect your discoveries from the chapter to the results you want to create.

- An **Experiment** that will only take you a few minutes but will help you further embed what you're learning and generate new insights.

- A **Web link** you can use to share your insights, connect with others and access videos and other learning materials.

The ultimate leverage point

This introduction started with the *number one result* question. As you've read, my *first* answer to this question initiated a chain of events that resulted in me sitting on the side of a ski slope, with sore feet and a troubled mind. But the subsequent transformation revealed a far more powerful answer to the question: a *new* leverage point that proved to be the key to creating the results that really matter to you and for you, and enjoying your relationships and your life more and more fully. In Part One of this book, you're going to be introduced to what I consider to be the *ultimate* leverage point. . .

Bottom line results: To grow your business results in a way that's healthy, fulfilling and sustainable, you and your team need to grow as individuals. The three transformations you'll be going through as you read this book represent the *ultimate leverage point* for your personal evolution; a framework for you to maximize the return on your investment of time, energy, money and other resources as you create the results that *truly* matter to you in a way that fits with your true nature.

keep exploring ⁘ connect with others
share your discoveries ⁘ deepen your understanding

Experiment: What's the number one result that – if you were to achieve it – you believe would have the biggest positive impact in your life? Ask yourself this question, or get someone else to ask you. You may come up with a number of different answers before settling on one that 'feels right'. Of course, your answer to this question is likely to change and evolve as you continue reading this book. It can be fun and interesting to make a note of what your answer is now, then compare it to the answer you give when you reach the end of the book (I'll ask the question again when we get there).

www.jamiesmart.com/resultsintro

PART ONE

GROUNDING
Your Personal
Transformation

*Without self knowledge, without understanding
the working and functions of his machine,
man cannot be free, he cannot govern himself
and he will always remain a slave.*

George Gurdjieff
Philosopher, composer, teacher

*The brain can only assume its proper behaviour
when consciousness is doing what it is
designed for: not writhing and whirling
to get out of present experience, but being
effortlessly aware of it.*

Alan Watts
Philosopher, author, speaker

1

You're Built for Reality; You're Optimized for Results

....

You are braver than you believe, stronger than you seem, and smarter than you think.

A.A. Milne, Novelist, poet, creator of Winnie-the-Pooh

'This system uses your innate capacities and instinctive abilities, developed over millions of years. . .'

I'd never thought of myself as a fighter, but I was hit by a sudden realization. . .

You're built for reality.
You're optimized for results.
You've evolved to survive, transform and thrive.

I was learning *Krav Maga*, a self-defence system that teaches you to respond effectively in dangerous situations. And why is it so effective? Because it runs on the 'operating system' of your *innate capacities and instincts*; pre-existing abilities that show up *automatically*, without you having to think about it consciously. I'd never thought of myself as a fighter, but I was introduced to the fighter that had been right there within me my whole life.

You're going to be introduced to the 'operating system' of your *innate capacities and instincts* for creating meaningful results and living a life you love. As you discover the results-creator that's been *right there within you* your whole life, your ability to get results is going to increase exponentially.

You're built for reality, with the factory settings for creating results. Over the past million years, nature has asked each of your ancestors a question: are you resilient enough, attractive enough and creative enough to survive to breeding age, have children and pass on your genetic material? The fact that you're here means the answer to that question was 'yes', millions of times in succession.

You are a state-of-the-art results-creator, tempered in the
furnace of millions of years of evolution.

And one of the most valuable gifts that helps you survive and thrive in reality is your innate capacity for realization and insight.

You have an innate capacity for realization and insight

A realization is a fresh new thought; an insight that brings your understanding more closely into alignment with the truth of some aspect of life. History has numerous examples of dramatic realizations that have changed the world, for instance. . .

- Isaac Newton's insights into the principle of gravity that transformed our understanding of the material world and paved the way for the Industrial Revolution.

- The realizations about 'invisible matter' on doctors' hands that prompted Ignaz Semmelweis' pioneering of antiseptic procedures.

- James Watson's breakthrough discovery of DNA's double-helix structure, leading to numerous modern-day applications including agriculture, pharmaceuticals and forensics.

Realizations reveal pre-existing facts about the reality you're built for

In each case, the realization revealed the existence of *pre-existing facts* about some aspect of life; principles or laws behind how life *already* works. And the fact that you're reading this means you've had countless realizations and insights in *your own life*. . .

For example: The moment you were born, you started learning about the implications of *gravity*; a pre-existing fact of life. As you started exploring this new domain, you effortlessly processed the megabytes of data pouring through your senses and had realizations about the *fact* of gravity. These realizations came *automatically*, without you even having to think about it consciously. By the time you could walk, you had a deep 'embodied understanding' of the implications of gravity; an understanding you developed *without even knowing you were doing it*.

You have an innate capacity for realization.
A realization brings you more closely into
alignment with reality.
The more aligned with reality you are, the more
effective you can be at creating results.

Realization is a natural function of your mind

You've had countless realizations and insights over the years. If you'd like a simple metaphor for this, look at the FedEx logo. There are two images, hiding in plain sight, contained within the logo: A white spoon (poetically concealed in the letter 'e' in the word 'Fed') and a white arrow (hidden between the 'E' and the 'x' in the word 'Ex'). These two images have always been part of the 'reality' of the logo. You may not have *noticed* them until now, but they've always been there. The mechanism that takes you from 'looking' to 'seeing' is *realization*; a hit of fresh new perception that arrives from *beyond* your existing model of reality. And once you've seen them, you'll never be able to un-see them. Your realization will have brought your understanding more closely into alignment with reality. Every time you see this logo going forward, you're going to be reminded of your innate capacity for realization, and the principles we're exploring in this book.

Figure 1.1:   The FedEx logo

You possess superpowers

Your innate capacity for realization is one of a number of 'superpowers' you possess; the *deep drivers* you benefited from as you learned to walk. As a toddler, your innate capacity for. . .

- **Direction** shows you a purpose and possibility that inspire and motivate you.

- **Resilience** enables you to take risks, recover and get back up every time you fall over.

- **Creativity** has you innovating different approaches and creating solutions to problems.

- **Authenticity** means you trust yourself and stay through your authentic desires.

- **Intuition** lets you know when to practice, when to rest and when to try something different.

- **Presence** keeps you close to reality; aware, insightful and learning rapidly.

- **Connection** allows you to be playful and loving, secure in yourself and your world.

- **Clarity** lets you play full-out, clear-minded and at the very edge of your abilities.

Practicality check: How is realizing I'm built for reality going to help me get results?

These *deep drivers* are your 'default settings'. As a little child, you used them instinctively, throwing yourself fully into your passions and enthusiasms without hesitation, fear of failure or criticism. These deep drivers are still there within you, ready to serve you in creating the results you desire. For the remainder of this book, we're going to be using the term 'clarity' as a shorthand for the innate capacity for results-creation and rich experience of life you were born with. Putting it simply, *Clarity plus Action equals Results*

CLARITY   plus   **ACTION**   equals   **RESULTS**

Figure 1.2:   The CLARITY® Results Model

You can remember this easily by using the acronym and metaphor 'CAR' (Clarity + Action = Results). The more deeply you understand the principles we're going to be exploring in this book, the more flexibly, creatively and enjoyably you're going to be able to create the experiences and results you want in your life.

Whatever your experience has been so far in life, you have good reason to be hopeful. You have these innate capacities and deep drivers within you. As you get a deeper understanding of the principles behind clarity, you're going to find these capacities and instincts showing up automatically, more and more of the time, without you having to think about it consciously.

So if we all have these innate capacities and instincts, what gets in the way? If we're all state-of-the-art results-creators, why is it so often a struggle to solve our problems or make changes? Why does it sometimes seem so challenging to get results?

Bottom line results: The ability to sense and respond to threats and opportunities is becoming increasingly important. You possess innate capacities that are the *deep drivers* of business success. Your (and your organization's) ability to sense, respond and create results is a function of your *realization* of those innate capacities.

keep exploring ⁘ connect with others
share your discoveries ⁘ deepen your understanding

Experiment: What are some of your more powerful insights, realizations and embodied understandings that are already making a big difference to you and for you?

www.jamiesmart.com/results1

2

The One and Only Way Your Mind Always Works

When you have eliminated all which is impossible, then whatever remains, however improbable, must be the truth.

Sir Arthur Conan Doyle, Doctor, novelist, creator of Sherlock Holmes

'I need a formula for how this transformation is going to work. . .'

Ian Selby and I were 45 minutes into the first morning of a three-day 1:1 coaching intensive. Ian runs *Timbawood*, a specialist manufacturing business whose purpose is to restore and preserve Britain's architectural heritage. It's a successful, fast-growing company, but Ian had hired me because he felt stuck. He couldn't move forward and get to where he wanted to be in his work, his relationships and his life in general. He wanted clarity of direction and the ability to create new results. He wanted to experience more connection and less conflict in his relationships. We made a short list of the problems he wanted to solve, the changes he wanted to make and the goals he wanted to achieve as a result of our work together. But before we'd even finished our first session, he started to get anxious and told me, 'I need a *formula* for how this transformation is going to work.'

Suddenly, I felt stuck too. I didn't *have* a formula. Ian had paid a large sum of money to work with me, and I wasn't going to be able to give him what he wanted! My heart started to sink as my head filled up with worrying scenarios. I'd been temporarily deceived by a trick of the mind. . .

A trick of the mind

The single biggest barrier to progress – and the cause of most frustration, stuckness and suffering – is an innocent and widespread *misunderstanding* about how our minds work. This trick of the mind is validated and reinforced by the media, politicians, teachers, employers, friends, relatives, self-help books and even our own perceptual systems. By the time you've finished this chapter, you will have discovered the one and only way your mind *always* works, and the simple trick of the mind that stops people creating the results that matter to them. As you start to 'see through' this false belief, you'll be waking up to your true power as a results-creator.

Your experience is being generated from within you, right now!

The human mind has an extraordinary job to do. Millions of bits of information arrive at our senses every second. Our minds process that data, combine it with information from our memory banks and weave a coherent and stable perceptual reality that we experience as 'real'. The mind-made perceptual reality we construct seems so real to us that we rarely question its validity. . .

Look around at the environment you're in. Your experience of everything you can see, hear, feel, taste and smell is being generated from *within you*, moment to moment (a process that neuroscientist and consciousness researcher Anil Seth describes as 'a controlled hallucination'). Even the things you can see and hear 'out there' are experiences being generated from within you (albeit with a live data-feed). It seems to us as though we look out through our eyes at a world 'out there', but our perception is less like looking through the lens of a camera and more like a projector or a set of virtual reality goggles. Please note: I'm not saying that everything 'out there' is being generated from within you; I'm saying that your *experience* of everything 'out there' is being generated from within you, using the power of THOUGHT: the reality principle.

THOUGHT: the reality principle

People think. The principle of THOUGHT refers to our innate capacity to generate a perceptual reality; an outer and inner world that we can see, hear, feel, taste and smell. This principle is also the source of the countless thoughts and perceptions that arise in the course of a day.

- You were born into the principle of THOUGHT just as you were born into the principle of gravity.

- You use the principle of THOUGHT, *automatically* and *effortlessly* to generate a coherent perceptual reality, moment to moment.

- You're always living in a THOUGHT-generated perceptual reality and experiencing it as an *actual* reality.

Reality check

'Thanks Professor', I hear you say, 'but so what? What difference does it make that I'm living in a THOUGHT-generated perceptual reality? I still get evicted if I don't pay the rent.' Here's the difference it makes:

Your THOUGHT-generated perceptual reality is like a pair of glasses that colours everything you see.

*Your feelings are giving you feedback about the <u>glasses</u>
you're wearing, <u>not</u> what you're looking at.*

Don't take my word for it; check your own experience. Have you
noticed how. . .

- When you feel irritated, it can seem like it's caused by whoever
  or whatever you're thinking about.

- When you feel grateful, it's easy to find things to be grateful for.

- When you feel down or low, it can appear like there are really
  good reasons for it.

- When you feel happy, it seems like there are really good reasons for that.

- When you feel stressed-out, it often seems like the causes are
  outside you.

In fact, sometimes the very situations or people which seem annoy-
ing or frustrating on one day can seem sweet or charming the next.
That's because your feelings are giving you feedback on THOUGHT
taking form in the moment, *not* whatever you're thinking about.

*Thinking and feeling are two sides of the same coin. . .
You're <u>always</u> living in the feeling of THOUGHT in the moment. . .
But it often <u>seems</u> like you're feeling something
<u>other than</u> THOUGHT.*

Moving from La-la Land to reality

This is the illusion that had me fooled when Ian said he needed a formula. Fortunately, I woke up to the fact that my feelings of anxiety and stuckness *weren't* telling me about my client, my abilities or my lack of a formula. . . My feelings were alerting me to the principle of THOUGHT taking an anxious form in the moment. The second I realized this, I fell out of the 'La-la Land' of my cluttered thinking and back into the present; back into the reality we're built for, where the solution suddenly came to me. I wrote on the whiteboard:

$$\text{You} + \text{Misunderstanding} = \text{Stuck}$$

I said, 'Your sense of being stuck is the result of a fundamental misunderstanding of where your experience is coming from. But your innate capacity for realization will help you see through that misunderstanding and wake up to a rich, fulfilling experience of life'.

Earlier in the session, Ian had told me that when he was a young man, he was very happy-go-lucky, spontaneous and carefree. As he grew older, he had become more serious and busy-minded. He longed for the sense of freedom, fun and happiness that he used to enjoy. I told him he was going to *love* the second part of the formula:

$$\text{You} - \text{Misunderstanding} = \begin{array}{l}\text{Clarity, Freedom, Fun,}\\ \text{Spontaneity, Fulfilment,}\\ \text{Love, Happiness, Results}\end{array}$$

'Great', Ian said. 'We've got the formula we need. Let's go'.

History has numerous examples of this kind of illusion:

Misunderstanding/Illusion/Trick of the mind/La-la Land	The reality you're built for/ Fact of life/Pre-existing truth
Flat earth	Spherical earth
Geocentric universe (earth is the unmoving centre)	Solar system (earth goes round the sun)
Stars and planets are held in place by crystal spheres	The principle of gravity
Infection is caused by miasmas, humours, moral character and other factors	Infection is caused by germs

Once again, you're a born results-creator. The primary obstacle to you creating the results that matter to you is the outside-in misunderstanding; the mistaken belief that you're feeling something *other than* THOUGHT in the moment. As you realize this for yourself, you'll start experiencing the unexpected yet inevitable results of living more closely in alignment with the reality you're built for.

Misunderstanding/Illusion/Trick of the mind/La-la Land	The reality you're built for/ Fact of life/Pre-existing truth
The outside-in misunderstanding: it honestly seems like your feelings are giving you feedback about something other than Thought in the moment, for example. . .	*The inside-out reality:* your feelings are giving you feedback about THOUGHT in the moment and *nothing else*

- Past events
- Future possibilities
- Current circumstances
- Other people
- Your skills, abilities and
  potentials
- What you're like as a person

Reality check

'I've seen the words "feeling" and "feelings" ten times already in this chapter. Is this a book about emotions?' No. The sentence 'You're living in the feeling of the principle of THOUGHT taking form in the moment' can be stated in a variety of ways. . .

- You're living in the *experience* of THOUGHT in the moment.

- You're living in a THOUGHT-generated perceptual reality.

- You're living in your moment-to-moment state of mind/ attitude/mindset/mood.

Your whole experience of life is a THOUGHT-generated totality; an undivided unity springing into being, moment by moment. There is no division between thinking and feeling, psychology and emotion. It is *one unified experience* being created using the power of THOUGHT.

Is this emotional intelligence?

The past 20 years have seen increasing interest in 'emotional intelligence' as an explanation for high performance in certain domains (e.g. leadership, negotiation, influence). Unfortunately, attempts to add the 'skills' of emotional intelligence to people's repertoire have often achieved only patchy results until now. Why? Because true emotional intelligence isn't *additive*; it's an expression of *innate capacities* that you already possess. The 'skills' of emotional intelligence emerge *naturally* when there's nothing getting in the way. And what gets in the way? Contaminated thinking arising from the outside-in misunderstanding. But as you *subtract* that misunderstanding, you're going to find the qualities of emotional intelligence emerging and developing *automatically* as you interact with others. This is the essence of subtractive psychology.

The power of subtraction

Over the next three days, I guided Ian through the discoveries we're going to be exploring together in this book. As he started to 'see through' the outside-in misunderstanding, he began to relax into his true nature, and wake up to the beauty of life. On the third day, we reviewed the list of outcomes Ian had made at the beginning, and he started laughing. As we went through his list of objectives, we found that each of the problems, changes and desired results looked profoundly different.

Problems	Changes	Desired results
The problem no longer existed, or. . .	The change no longer seemed impor-tant, or. . .	The result no longer seemed impor-tant, or. . .
The solution was now obvious, and he felt capable and motivated to resolve the problem, or. . .	The change had already hap-pened, or. . .	The result had been replaced by some-thing much more inspiring and natural for him, or. . .
The urgency was gone, and he felt comfortable and con-fident that the solu-tion would emerge in due course.	The urgency was gone, and he was happy to let it emerge in an organic way.	The way forward was obvious, and he felt ready and excited to start creating it.

I love this part of the transformation process. As you fall out of the La-la Land of your misunderstanding, you come to rest in the reality of clarity, freedom and possibility. As you start waking up to your true nature, you realize just how much power you have to live a life that deeply inspires you.

In the time since our three days together, Ian's life and business have continued to transform. As well as a new sense of energy and personal direction, he's enjoying deeper-than-ever connections in his relationships, and more fun and spontaneity in general. As Ian has introduced this understanding into his business, it's had a dramatic effect on his team and their performance. In the 24 months since Ian's intensive, his business has gone from being 'stuck' to experiencing an impressive 60% growth. He told me, 'It's wonderful to see my team flourish, take on more responsibility and be so much more productive. We're connected, aligned and all pulling in the same direction. For me personally, this shows up in my life as working less for more results.' Very importantly, he no longer feels stuck, and is enjoying sharing his new-found clarity with clients, colleagues and loved ones. And the formula I came up with for Ian ended up being boiled down to *The Clarity Equation*. . .

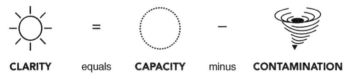

CLARITY equals **CAPACITY** minus **CONTAMINATION**

Figure 2.1: The CLARITY® Equation

Practicality check: How is a deeper understanding of my mind going to help me get results?

This simple formula, *Clarity equals Capacity minus Contamination*, points us back to the innate capacities and deep drivers we talked about in Chapter 1. . .

- **Capacity**: You have an innate capacity for wellbeing, realization, resilience and high performance. You're built for reality and optimized for results.

- **Contamination**: The only thing that ever obscures this capacity is contaminated thinking, arising from the outside-in misunderstanding.

- **Clarity**: As you wake up from that misunderstanding and get more closely aligned with reality, clarity emerges.

As you experience greater clarity in your life, you're going to have realizations and insights into what results matter to you and for you. You'll also have greater access to your innate capacities for bringing those results into being while enjoying the process.

As you get greater clarity, you'll find problems dissolving, solutions emerging and new desires being awakened. As you start to see a bigger picture of what's possible for you, you'll be getting opportunities to let go of some excess baggage. . .

Bottom line results: High performance is a strong predictor of business success. A clear mind is *essential* for high performance, yet we're living at a time when our mental clarity is under attack from smartphones, social media and spam. But here's the thing: your mood is like a pair of glasses; your feelings are telling you about the glasses you're wearing, *not* what you're looking at. Seeing through the outside-in misunderstanding is the quickest, most effective way to enjoy a clear mind, more of the time, with high levels of connection, motivation and performance.

keep exploring ⋅:⋅ connect with others
share your discoveries ⋅:⋅ deepen your understanding

Experiment: What are some of your more impactful and liberating realizations and insights so far in your life? What are some of the examples you can identify where your innate capacity for realization has brought you more closely into alignment with reality? Take a few moments to reflect on the fact that this power for realization is one of the most valuable gifts you possess, even if you haven't recognized it until now.

www.jamiesmart.com/results2

3

Eliminating Worry, Anxiety and Fear of Criticism

....

The less you fear, the more power you will have.

Curtis Jackson (aka 50 Cent), Musician,
entrepreneur, actor, producer

'It's as though a lifetime of limiting beliefs and negative ideas about myself have just fallen away. . .'

Donna Churchman had been terrified of public speaking for as long as she could remember. Despite being very accomplished (Donna's an award-winning designer), she felt extremely anxious speaking to large groups. I wasn't aware of this until she had an earth-shaking insight on the first weekend of my coach training programme. She told me, 'It's as though a lifetime of limiting beliefs and negative ideas about myself have just fallen away.' She'd seen through the illusion of her extreme anxiety.

Worry, anxiety and fear of criticism are 'optical illusions of the mind', with no more reality than a daydream or a highway mirage. As you start seeing them for what they are, you further harness your ability to create results.

So what do I mean by 'optical illusions of the mind'?

The teddy bear factor

Small children often have a teddy bear or security blanket. If the child 'bonds' with the teddy bear, it soon seems like the bear is a source of peace and security. But this is a trick of the mind – 100% of the feelings of peace and security are generated from within the child. The bear is neutral. If the teddy gets left behind when the family goes on holiday, it seems like the *absence* of the bear is the source of their feelings of anxiety. But this *too* is a trick of the mind. 100% of the feelings are coming from within the child.

This example is uncontroversial, but how quickly do we change our tune when we substitute the 'adult teddy bears' of money, jobs or romantic partners? Of our future hopes, fears or uncertainties? Of our past victories, defeats or indiscretions? How different does it seem when we ponder the 'teddy bear' of our physical body, our health or our personality? 100% of your feelings of worry, anxiety and insecurity are generated from within you, even when it *seems like* they're coming from an 'adult teddy bear'. The same goes for your feelings of peace, security and comfort. The teddy bear is always neutral.

It appears as though the sun rises, but it's an illusion caused by the rotation of the earth. It seems like our feelings of security come from our income, our relationships or our teddy bears, but it's an illusion caused by our perception. Of course, this doesn't just apply to our feelings of security; it also holds true for feelings of *insecurity*.

Misunderstanding/Illusion/Trick of the mind/La-la Land	The reality you're built for/Fact of life/Pre-existing truth
The outside-in misunderstanding: It honestly *seems* like your feelings are giving you feedback about something *other than* THOUGHT in the moment, for example. . . – Some future event or outcome (worry and anxiety tend to be future-oriented) – What you're like as a person (self-doubt, shame and shyness tend to be self-oriented) – Past occurrences (guilt, regret and remorse tend to be past-oriented) – Other people (resentment, envy and jealousy tend to be other-oriented)	*The inside-out reality:* Your feelings are giving you feedback about THOUGHT in the moment and *nothing else*. 100% of your feelings are an experience of 100% of your THOUGHT-generated perceptual reality. 0% of your feelings are an experience of anything *other than* THOUGHT in the moment

The *illusion* that tricks us into believing our felt experience is being generated from something *other than* THOUGHT is both compelling and *invisible*. We all get fooled by it. There's no immunity from this trick of the mind. There is, however, an inoculation. . .

> *As you continue to deepen your understanding of the principles behind clarity, you'll be tricked less often and wake up more quickly when you <u>do</u> get tricked.*

Why feelings of worry or anxiety are not the problem

Everyone sometimes experiences feelings of insecurity, such as worry, anxiety or self-doubt. That's not a problem. Those feelings are giving you feedback on the *totality* of your THOUGHT-generated experience in the moment, and that's really *useful*. The problem is that you sometimes believe your feelings are letting you know about something *other than* THOUGHT.

> *Your feelings are a reflection of THOUGHT in the moment and nothing else.*

Feelings are *impersonal*. Our feelings don't know anything about our past, our future, our circumstances, other people or what we're like. When we mistakenly believe our feelings are letting us know about something *other than* THOUGHT in this moment, we've slipped into La-la Land.

We sometimes believe we're in La-la Land

'La-la Land' is a nickname for a world that people believe in, but that doesn't actually exist. Some are literary, such as Narnia, Discworld and Middle Earth. Some are scientific, such as the geocentric model (astronomy before Copernicus), miasmas (medicine before germ theory) and the flat earth. But they're all fictional.

When we believe in a La-la Land, we're believing the world works in a way that is not based in reality. We've slipped into misunderstanding and contaminated thinking. And here's the thing:

You're not built for a non-existent La-la Land. . .
You're built for reality.

The fact that you understand the reality of germs means you wash your hands regularly and cover your mouth when you cough. These behaviours are grounded in a better understanding of reality than people who lived 200 years ago had. As a result of having a better understanding of *how life already works*, you get to prosper, thrive and be healthy. Your understanding is aligned more closely with the reality you're built for.

When you're 'hanging out in reality', your innate capacities are fully available to you. You get intuitions about when to take action and when to rest. You have a natural capacity for connection, insight and realization. But it's a little harder to come by when you're hanging out in La-la Land. The moment a person believes that they're feeling something other than THOUGHT in the moment, they've stepped into an illusory non-reality; a world that doesn't exist. It's tough to get results there!

But here's the best bit. You *already* live in reality and you always have done. The outside-in non-reality is a dream, an illusion, a fantasy world. The only place La-la Land exists is in our heads. In reality, all is well, and you have everything you need to respond powerfully in the moment.

Once again:

> *Feelings are giving you <u>essential</u> feedback about THOUGHT in the moment; the glasses you're wearing. . . That's not a problem. The problem is that we sometimes believe our feelings are letting us know about something <u>other than</u> the glasses we're wearing. . .*

Reality check

'Wait a minute. I've read that depression is caused by chemical and hormonal imbalances. Are you really saying that stress, anxiety and depression are just a person's thinking?'

Yes and no. . .

Consider someone who blushes in embarrassment as a colleague tells a suggestive joke. Blushing is the end result of a variety of involuntary processes. These involve neurological activity, stress hormones, neurochemicals, blood vessel dilation etc. And what causes all of this?

THOUGHT in the moment. . .

Their non-blushing colleagues are having a different Thought-generated experience, so they don't blush.

Think about it: If something as simple as 'embarrassed thinking' can have such a profound impact on a person's brain and body (i.e. blushing), what do you think the impact of months or years of 'depressed thinking' will have had on a person's brain chemistry?

While it's possible that differences in brain chemistry and genetics have an influence on a person's state of mind, we won't be able to determine the relationship *definitively* until research is conducted by scientists who have an understanding of the nature of THOUGHT. Until that point, it's likely that 'symptoms' and 'correlations' will continue to be misinterpreted as 'causes'.

In fact, a 2013 paper by Brett J. Deacon, PhD (published in the highly regarded *Clinical Psychology Review: The Future of Evidence-Based Practice in Psychotherapy**) raises significant concerns about the biomedical model. He suggests that framing mental disorders as biochemically-induced brain diseases, then treating them with 'disease-specific' psychiatric medications has led to a lack of clinical innovation, and poor results for patients. Deacon states that 'an honest and public dialog about the validity and utility of the bio-medical paradigm is urgently needed'.

*SOURCE: The biomedical model of mental disorder: A critical analysis of its validity, utility, and effects on psychotherapy research by Brett J. Deacon PhD. *Clinical Psychology Review* Volume 33, Issue 7, November 2013, Pages 846–861

When we slip into the La-la Land of the outside-in misunder-standing, we go into 'victim' mode. Our thinking accelerates and multiplies as we mistakenly attribute our feelings to exter-nal factors. But the moment we wake up to the fact of where our experience is coming from, our heads start to clear, and we fall back into the reality of the now.

Practicality check: How is eliminating worry, anxiety and fear of criticism going to help me get results?

As you get a deeper understanding of the principles behind clarity, it's going to take things *off* your mind and bring your innate capaci-ties to the fore. You'll find yourself having more and more freedom to take the actions you need to create the results that matter to you.

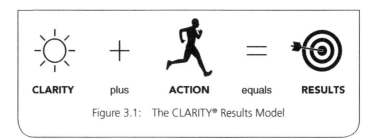

Figure 3.1:   The CLARITY® Results Model

Speak to 100 people like you're speaking to one person

On the day of her realization, Donna stood up and talked to the 40-person coach training group about what she'd seen. A few months after that, she gave an online masterclass called 'Speak to 100 people like you're speaking to one person'. She now works helping creative professionals understand the principles behind clarity. Two years after her insight, Donna flew to Berlin and gave a presentation about these principles to 350 of the world's leading creatives at the ProMaxBDA Conference. She was amazed at how enjoyable she found it once she realized she could express herself, free from worry and anxiety.

As you see through the illusion of worry, anxiety and self-doubt, you open a space to create results.

So what fills the space left by these optical illusions of the mind?

Bottom line results: Stress, worry, anxiety, frustration and fear of criticism are like sand in the gears of any organization, reducing productivity and driving counterproductive behaviour. But as you see through the trick of the mind that gives rise to them, you free yourself to give your best, set an encouraging example for others and focus on results that matter.

keep exploring ∴ connect with others
share your discoveries ∴ deepen your understanding

Experiment: Go to the sales counter in a retail store and make an absurd request with a straight face. Examples include asking for lingerie in a butcher's shop, perfume in a toyshop or pizza in a bank. If the thought of this has your heart pounding. . . where do you believe those feelings are coming from?

www.jamiesmart.com/results3

4

The Source of Resourcefulness, Resilience and Results

....

Most people tiptoe through life, hoping to make it safely to death.

Earl Nightingale, Author, speaker, radio personality

'I had this big epiphany the day of the earthquake. . .'

Mahima doesn't remember where she flicked through my first book, *CLARITY*, but a phrase stuck in her mind. . . '100% of your feelings come from THOUGHT in the moment'. Not long after that, the massive April 2015 Nepal earthquake hit (Mahima is a crisis management consultant who lives in Kathmandu, 50 miles from the epicentre). The earthquake destroyed buildings, killing thousands, and for the first few hours, Mahima was terrified. Then she had a sudden realization:

> *Your felt experience is a reflection of* THOUGHT, *not your circumstances. In this moment you are as safe as you are ever going to be and as safe as you have ever been.*

As Mahima's fear evaporated, she found that she was more engaged with life, not less. She was more capable and resourceful; able to give her all to the situation, secure in the knowledge that she'd be able to handle it, whatever happened. Mahima had woken up to her inner self; her true nature.

You're capable of far more than you think, because you *are* far more than you think. You're about to get a deeper understanding of your true nature – the source of resourcefulness, resilience and results.

How often do you say 'I am'?

Think about some of the 'I am' statements you use (e.g. I am a man, I am a woman, I am single, I am married, I am stupid, I am clever, I am bad, I am good, I am stressed, I am peaceful, I am bored, I am tired, I am energized etc).

You can think of this sense of 'I am' like a light that illuminates whatever we shine it on. When a person says, 'I am Alex', 'I am stuck' or 'I am confident', it's similar to an equal sign, creating an equation in our perception that goes something like this:

$$I = Alex$$
$$I = Stuck$$
$$I = Confident$$

Once we've shone that sense of 'I am' on one of these concepts, it can really feel as though that's who or what we really are. But who you *really* are isn't your name, an emotion or some other label. Who you *really* are is that sense of 'I am'.

You are not what you think; you are the thinker.
You are not what the light is shining on; you are the light.

We're going to be referring to the light of 'I am' as CONSCIOUSNESS.

CONSCIOUSNESS: **the experience principle**

The principle of CONSCIOUSNESS refers to our capacity to have an *experience* of THOUGHT taking form in the moment. CONSCIOUSNESS brings our THOUGHT-generated experiential reality to life.

Sydney Banks was a Scottish welder who had a profound enlightenment experience in 1974, and realized there are principles behind human psychology (just as there are principles in the fields of physics or chemistry). He once said, "If you're searching for happiness; if you're searching for tranquility. . . if you're searching just to have a nice, peaceful, loving, understanding life. . . in actual fact, you're searching for your inner self."

Whatever you may <u>believe</u> you've been searching
for until now,
what you've <u>really</u> been seeking is your inner self. . .
What you've been looking <u>for</u>, you've been
looking <u>with</u>. . .
You are the light. . .

Your wellbeing

As a little child, you likely spent much of your time in a peaceful, contented state of mind. While you often felt bothered temporarily, you always returned to that place of peace and connection with your inner self; your wellbeing. I'll say that again: Your well *being*. . . the *well being* that you truly are.

Then somewhere along the way, we were trained to believe that admission to that place of peace and connection had to be earned, bought or achieved.

We were conditioned to look outside ourselves for the peace, happiness and security that can only be found within.

When you're looking to something *outside* yourself for a sense of peace, security or happiness, you're actually trying to find your inner self. And when you're concerned that your peace, security or happiness is at threat from something outside of you, you're believing that it could *stop* you finding your inner self.

The moment you realize that you already have what you've been searching for until now, you step into a different world. You'll still have results you're inspired to create, and you may use goals, targets or other objectives to achieve them, but where you're 'coming from' – the *feeling* you're living in – is entirely different. . .

You already are what you've been searching for until now. . . What you've been searching for, you've been searching with.

IMPLICATION: You can't be a victim of circumstance

Misunderstanding/Illusion/ Trick of the mind/La-la Land	The reality you're built for/ Fact of life/Pre-existing truth
The outside-in misunderstanding: it can honestly seem as though you are, have been or could be a victim of circumstance. The outside-in illusion can be so compelling that we sometimes feel certain that external circumstances, past occurrences or future events could cause us to feel a certain way	*The inside-out reality:* at the level of principle, it's not possible for you to be a victim of circumstance. Please note: I'm not saying it's not possible for stuff to *happen* to people. I might get a broken leg or a punch in the nose before today is over; it's *definitely* possible for stuff to happen to people. But it's not possible for any of those things to have a particular *emotional impact*. It's not possible for anything in the world of form to have a specific emotional impact. It's not possible for anything in the outside world to damage or harm you psychologically

You are psychologically safe

You're always living in the feeling of THOUGHT in the moment and always have been, even if you hadn't realized it until now. For the rest of your life, you're never going to feel anything *other than* THOUGHT in the moment. And there's no thinking that can harm you.

This is beautiful because it means you have the ultimate protection. It means you're *psychologically* safe from harm or attack.

Reality check

I'm not talking about physical safety – I definitely recommend you wear your seat belt and take appropriate steps to take care of your physical body. But psychologically, it's not possible for you to be harmed.

It's possible for people to *believe* the earth is flat, but that doesn't mean it actually *is* flat. Similarly, it's possible for us to *believe* we're victims of circumstance, but you can't actually *be* a victim of circumstance. And as you wake up to the fact of this, you start experiencing greater freedom, clarity and wellbeing.

Practicality check: How is realizing my true nature going to help me get results?

As you fall out of contaminated thinking, you come to rest in your inner self. . .

> *Your inner self is the source of all security,*
> *resilience and courage. . .*
> *Of all insight, realization and creativity. . .*
> *Of all passion, purpose and direction. . .*
> *Of all peace, love and connection. . .*

> *Of evolution and transformation. . .*
> *Your inner self is the source of all results.*
>
> Your inner self is the source of all results. As you wake up to who you really are, your capacity to create the results that matter to you increases exponentially.

The presence of sanity

I was interviewing Mahima (she was a scholarship student on the *Clarity Coach Training Programme*), when one of the other students asked if she'd taught these principles to other earthquake-survivors. Mahima replied that she hadn't taught them *explicitly*, but that the presence of sane human beings has a positive effect in its own right. She later wrote, 'In the eight months since the earthquake in Nepal, I have seen the broad and all-pervasive relevance of these principles. An understanding of the foundational principles behind how we function as human beings and 'how life works' changes everything from career planning and good governance to crisis response and parenting. It takes us beyond trauma and problem-solving to experiencing the full spectrum of a rich human life.'

The presence of sane human beings has a positive effect in its own right.

You are already mentally healthy; psychologically whole and resilient. The source of emotional intelligence is already right there within you. The only thing that *ever* gets in the way is the mistaken belief that we're feeling something *other than* THOUGHT in the moment. We each have mental health and wellbeing at our core, with the wisdom and common sense to make good decisions. So how do you know what to want?

Bottom line results: As you become more deeply acquainted with 'who you really are', you start freeing yourself from the delusion that your happiness, security and wellbeing are dependent on (or can be threatened by) your job, your results or your ambitions. Paradoxically, as you *subtract* that delusion, your increasing clarity releases huge amounts of energy for you to enjoy your current circumstances, while focusing your energies on creating the results that matter to you.

| CLARITY | plus | ACTION | equals | RESULTS |

Figure 4.1: The CLARITY® Results Model

keep exploring ⁂ connect with others
share your discoveries ⁂ deepen your understanding

Experiment: Say 'I am <your name>', either aloud or to yourself. Notice whatever sense of 'I am-ness' you become aware of. You have a name, but you are not your name; you're the one who is experiencing this name. You have a body, but you are not your body; you're the one who is experiencing this body. You have many thoughts, but you are not your thoughts; you're the one who is experiencing these thoughts. I encourage you to reflect on the notion that who you <u>really</u> are is that formless, indestructible and ever-present purity of 'I am'. . .the principle of Consciousness.

www.jamiesmart.com/results4

5

Finding Your Place of Meaning, Passion and Purpose

....

If you don't know where you're going. . .
Any road will take you there. . .

George Harrison, Musician, film producer

'What's your purpose in life?'

I was attending a workshop in 2007 when we were asked this question. I trotted out an 'official purpose' I'd come up with a few months earlier, but it no longer rang true. I shook my head, saying, 'That doesn't feel right; I have to be true to myself.' In that moment, wisdom was speaking. . .

You have to be true to yourself.
This is your purpose right now; to be true to yourself.
To be guided by intuition, realization and authentic desire.

While I'd been looking *outside* myself, trying to figure out some suitably grand purpose, the voice of the *inner* self was speaking the simple fact of my purpose in that moment. . . *You have to be true to yourself.* You see, it turns out that you don't find your *purpose*; purpose finds *you*. In this chapter, you're going to be getting in touch with your inner source of evolutionary purpose.

Exponential organizations and the power of purpose

While researching his ground-breaking book, *Exponential Organizations*, angel investor Salim Ismail and his team explored businesses that were growing at an exponential rate (doubling every year). One of the qualities they all share is a 'massive transformational purpose' (MTP), for instance. . .

- TED's MTP is to spread ideas.

- Uber's MTP is to evolve the way the world moves.

- Kickstarter's MTP is to help bring creative projects to life.

- LinkedIn's MTP is to create economic opportunity for every member of the global workforce.

- Google's MTP is to organize the world's information and make it universally accessible and useful.

Millennials are flocking to purpose-driven companies. Research shows that purpose-oriented employees are far more likely to be high performers, with strong levels of engagement and loyalty to the purpose-driven organizations that employ them.

Your inner source of evolutionary purpose

While you may not be founding an exponential-growth business, a sense of purpose and direction are innate; as natural to you as breathing. When you were a child, a purpose would find you, captivate you and guide you until you transcended it. This is the sense of evolutionary purpose that has already motivated you. . .

- To crawl, to walk and to talk.

- To explore the world and learn about what fascinates you.

- To throw yourself into pastimes, hobbies and other activities.

- To develop skills and master them.

A purpose finds you, captivates you, then guides you until you transcend it.

That sense of evolutionary purpose is what has me writing this book, and may well be what has you reading it. Stop and consider that for a moment. Are you open to the possibility that your innate capacity for purpose and direction is guiding you *in this very moment*?

So what gets in the way of realizing your purpose?

You may have been told you need to 'find your purpose', but how do you do that? It turns out that a more valuable question to ask is, 'What gets in the way of your *realizing* purpose?' What gets in the way is looking for it where it isn't. . .

> *The misguided search for purpose is the biggest obstacle to finding it.*

It turns out there's only one thing that ever gets in the way of you knowing what's right for you in the moment: contaminated thinking. The source of contaminated thinking is the outside-in misunderstanding; the mistaken belief that you're feeling something *other than* THOUGHT in the moment.

> *Your feelings don't know anything about your character, your circumstances or your sense of direction.*
> *Your feelings only ever know about THOUGHT in the moment.*

You can't find something where it isn't

If purpose was a physical object, then losing it and looking for it would make sense, but it isn't. Purpose is a realization that brings you closer to the reality of life that you're part of.

Imagine a whirlpool in a fast-flowing river. While you could name the whirlpool and describe its characteristics, it has no existence independent of the river. While you can *perceive* the whirlpool as distinct and separate for practical purposes, it is never *actually* separate. The whirlpool is inseparable from the river, part of an undivided whole.

*While you have a name and can describe your characteristics,
you have no existence independent of the oneness of life.
While you can perceive yourself as distinct and separate
for practical purposes, you are never <u>actually</u> separate.
You are inseparable from the intelligence and oneness
of life, part of an undivided whole.*

MIND: The power principle

The principle of MIND is the 'intelligent energy' that shows up in all aspects of the natural world. MIND is the 'power source' behind life. Various cultures and fields have different names for this power: Life force, universal energy, chi, nature, the great spirit, God, the no-thing, evolution, random chance etc. You can think of it in whatever way makes sense to you.

We'll be referring to the oneness of life as the principle of MIND. You, your life and your purpose in the moment are all an expression of this formless principle.

So what is 'purpose'?

Purpose is a thought, and like all thoughts, it comes with a feeling. Your evolutionary purpose is less likely to be something you 'figure out' so much as something you glimpse or *realize*; a function of your innate capacity for insight. When you have such a realization, it may have some of these qualities. . .

- It may come with a feeling of gentle certainty or knowing.

- It may come as a sudden flash of realization, or as a slow awakening.

- It may strike you as extremely obvious, with an 'Of course! How did I not see this before?' quality.

So how do you create the conditions for this kind of realization?

Stop looking for it where it isn't.

When we look outside ourselves for that which can only be found within us, it sets up an 'outside-in' dynamic that generates contaminated thinking. But when we *subtract* that misunderstanding, our innate capacities emerge. Here's a slightly expanded version of *The Clarity Equation*.

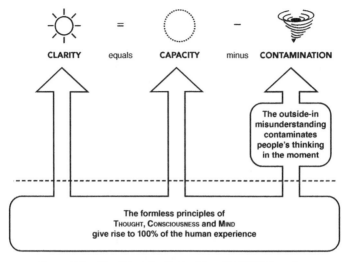

Figure 5.1:   The Principles Behind The CLARITY® Equation

A paradigm for psychology

MIND, THOUGHT and CONSCIOUSNESS are the principles behind human psychological functioning, first articulated by Sydney Banks. While they're pointing in the same direction as many wisdom traditions of the past, Banks was able to go further, stating them as 'principles' in the scientific sense of the word (i.e. fundamental laws of reality such as the principle of gravity). Whenever humanity discovers the foundational principles behind a field, it creates a shared basis of agreement for future explorations which then *transforms* that field.

The shared basis for agreement is referred to as the field's 'paradigm'.

- Newton's *realization* of the principle of gravity formed the basis for a paradigm that transformed the field of physics.

- Lavoisier's *realization* of the principles behind combustion formed the basis for a paradigm that transformed the field of chemistry.

- Semmelweis' *realization* of germ theory formed the basis for a paradigm that transformed the field of medicine.

Sydney Banks insightfully realized and articulated the foundational principles behind psychology; principles that form the basis of a paradigm for a field that has been awash with conflicting ideas, concepts and theories until now. Banks' discovery is at the heart of *subtractive psychology*.

- Banks' realization of the principles behind human psychological functioning form the basis for a paradigm that will transform the field of psychology.

Purpose can give you a glimpse of the future

In late 2008, I was feeling off-track, frustrated and directionless. Then, I started exploring the principles behind clarity. As my understanding deepened, my head started to clear and

I had a series of realizations. The first realization came to me while I was asleep and dreaming. . .

Everything you've been looking for <u>outside</u> of you is actually to be found <u>within</u> you.
External results can be wonderful, but they can't give you a feeling.

I awoke with a start, feeling better than I could remember feeling in months. I'd suddenly realized that peace, security and fulfilment can never be found in external circumstances and accomplishments. While external results can be *wonderful*, they can't give you a feeling; that can only come from *within* you. The second realization arrived a few weeks later. . .

The fact that you can perceive <u>anything</u> means you have the source of peace, fulfilment and wellbeing already within you.

This shocked me, and had an immediate impact on my work with clients. When you know with absolute certainty that a person is fundamentally OK, it influences how you experience that person and how they experience you.

The third insight arrived a month after that, and revealed something truly extraordinary. You see, purpose can give you a glimpse of a possible future.

Practicality check: How is understanding purpose going to help me get results?

As purpose finds you, it becomes easier to make decisions about how to invest your time, energy and other resources. When you authentically share your purpose with others, it's like you become a tuning fork. People who resonate with you are drawn to you and your message. The *feeling* of purpose and direction is a powerful energy in its own right, and can awaken courage, motivation and resolve.

Bottom line results: A felt sense of purpose can inspire passion, loyalty and motivation in the people who resonate with it. Purpose-oriented employees are far more likely to be high performers, with strong levels of engagement. As you become more attuned to the subtle signals of purpose, you'll find yourself tapping into its power for yourself and others, more and more easily.

*keep exploring ⋅:⋅ connect with others
share your discoveries ⋅:⋅ deepen your understanding*

Experiment: Open to the possibility that you've already been guided by a sense of purpose and direction your whole life. You started with learning to crawl, walk and talk. At some points you may have been very aware of the guiding hand of purpose; at other points less so. What would happen if you were to experiment with letting go of the search for purpose, and relaxing into the knowledge that it's already guiding you perfectly?

www.jamiesmart.com/results5

6

Leadership: The Inner Key to Confidence and Certainty

....

*You don't need to put the yolk in the egg.
The yolk is already in the egg.*

Valda Monroe, Educator, single-paradigm pioneer

'These principles are to psychology what the discovery of germs was to medicine. . .'

It was the spring of 2009, and I'd been exploring the principles behind clarity for six months. I'd seen big changes in my own life and in the lives of my clients. But until that morning, I'd been relating to these principles as an additive approach; yet another tool for my toolbox. The sudden realization that these were actually *principles* – fundamental laws of reality – changed everything. . .

The principles behind clarity represent the future of psychology. . .
These principles are to psychology what the discovery of germs was to medicine.

I suddenly knew I was going to be exploring and sharing these principles for the next 20 years. Just as the acceptance of germ theory had transformed the *physical* health of humanity, the widespread realization of these principles would transform the *psychological* health of humanity. Purpose had found me and given me a glimpse of the future. My priorities changed in a heartbeat; it was clear what I had to do. . . 'You have to get a deeper understanding of these principles, and start sharing them with people'.

And that's when I started feeling insecure. An explosion of thoughts crowded into my mind. . .

- Who did I think I was, claiming to know the future of psychology? I'd dropped out of university and didn't even have a *degree*.

- Why just 20 years? If I was serious about it, surely I would be committed to doing this for the rest of my life.

- Who was I to be telling people they had the source of security, wisdom and wellbeing already within them? I was a habitual worrier, with a variety of personal issues.

Fortunately, I was no stranger to the feelings of insecurity that often follow on the heels of inspiration. By the time you've finished this chapter, you'll be more in touch with your *inner* source of leadership; the key to courage, confidence and certainty.

When are you a leader?

'What are some of the times and situations in your life when you've shown up as a leader?' I've asked this question to countless participants on my workshops and programmes. At first, some people sometimes protest that they don't have any examples. But before long, their leadership stories emerge. . .

- The teenage boy who saved his brother from choking while their mother watched helplessly.

- The intern whose stroke of insight saved their company tens of thousands of pounds.

- The young girl who stepped in when another child was being picked on and stared the bullies down.

They often say, 'I didn't think of that as being a leader; it just seemed *obvious*', but that statement reveals the *essence* of leadership.

*When we're caught up in contaminated thinking, we look
to others, trying to figure out what to do.
When you've got nothing on your mind, your innate
leadership qualities emerge effortlessly.
When you're hanging out in reality, leadership is
common sense.*

DISTINCTION: Additive approaches vs subtractive understanding

In his provocative book, *Antifragile*, risk analyst Nassim Nicholas Taleb explains that we tend to be suckers for the **additive approaches** offered by how-to books, crash diets, get-rich-quick schemes etc. For a simple example, look at the 'top tips' articles featured on the covers of popular magazines. . .

- The 5 keys to six-pack abs
- The 7 tips for finding Mr Right

- The 5 keys to financial freedom
- 7 career moves to make you unbeatable

- The 6 secrets of successful relationships
- 7 steps to a swimsuit body

When people are looking for additive approaches, they're asking the question, 'What do I need to add to my life/myself/my skills/my personality to make me more X and less Y?' The structure of the additive approach is always the same:

You + Additive Approach = Super You

This seductive and compelling promise is like crack cocaine to our insecurities. It's the driver behind the billions of dollars made from 'success', 'get rich quick' and 'how to x, y, z fast' materials each year. It's why those magazines can put new tips on every cover. When we're feeling insecure, we're compelled by the notion of an additive approach. But there's a problem. . .

Additive approaches rarely work

In practice, additive approaches rarely deliver the hoped-for results, and can even cause actual harm. In the USA, it's estimated that illness caused accidentally by medical interventions is *the third biggest killer* after heart disease and cancer. The 2012 arrest of 200 UK gang leaders under the banner of the government's 'all-out war on gangs and gang culture' resulted in even more ruthless youngsters jockeying for position. When you read the seven top tips, they instantly strike you as obvious ('Why didn't I think of that?') and are often forgotten the next instant. Why?

> *Additive advice without embodied understanding has little or no effect.*

Doctors and nurses in the 1800s had to be *forced* to wash their hands, because they didn't have an understanding of germ theory. Once you understand the reality of germs, washing your hands is just common sense. *Until* you understand the reality of germs, it's just one more chore on an already long list.

Subtraction is the secret of leadership

The secret to leading yourself and others is subtraction. As I mentioned in Chapter 3, the CLARITY® model is ruthlessly *subtractive* (hence the term *subtractive psychology*).

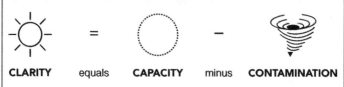

CLARITY   equals   **CAPACITY**   minus   **CONTAMINATION**

Figure 6.1:   The CLARITY® Equation

Clarity is your natural state of mind; your innate leadership qualities emerge effortlessly when there's no contaminated thinking getting in the way. When people first see this, they typically look for another additive approach, and ask 'OK, how do I get rid of my contaminated thinking?' Surprisingly, the answer to this question isn't addition, but *subtraction*. Here's a more leveraged question: 'What's been giving rise to the contaminated thinking in the first place?' After all, if we can identify the 'cause' of that thinking, we can address *that* and cut it off at the source! So what's the cause?

Misunderstanding contaminates

To answer that question, let's use physical health as an analogy. The human body has an incredible capacity for healing wounds, as long as the wound is free from contamination by germs and bacteria. In the 1830s, surgeons innocently infected their patients by operating on them with dirty scalpels in filthy operating theatres. Surgeons had a misunderstanding about the cause of infection, and that mis-understanding gave rise to countless unintentional contaminations. Similarly, our misunderstanding of the cause of our experience ('the outside-in misunderstanding') gives rise to the 'contaminant' of overthinking.

Understanding is subtractive

Subtracting a misunderstanding, and getting more closely aligned with reality, has a profound effect. Ignaz Semmelweis' insights about the nature of germs and bacteria have resulted in a 30-year increase in the average lifespan of every person on the planet. See-ing through this misunderstanding about how life *already works* has had a bigger effect on physical wellbeing than *all medical interventions combined.*

The harmful effects of the outside-in misunderstanding are infi-nitely more devastating than the combined benefits of every tech-nique, methodology or psychiatric medication ever developed. Seeing through the outside-in misunderstanding can provide enor-mous psychological benefit. And as your psychology is behind all your decisions, performances and results, the impact on your life as a whole can be truly profound.

You – Misunderstanding = Super You

Getting a deeper understanding of the principles behind clarity unlocks your innate leadership qualities. . . The source of confidence, certainty and results.

The deep drivers are your innate leadership qualities

The symptoms of the common cold (e.g. coughing and sneezing) are caused by a virus. When you have the virus, the symptoms emerge effortlessly. So what's the cause that gives rise to the symptoms of leadership? The formless principles of Mind, Consciousness and Thought. These principles create 100% of your moment-to-moment experience. When contaminated thinking is subtracted, they show up as the eight deep drivers we mentioned in Chapter 1. These innate qualities are the source of emotional intelligence and authentic leadership. . .

Direction: A sense of direction, purpose and motivation, free from urgency and undue pressure.

Resilience: A strong sense of inner resilience, security and trust in yourself in life.

Creativity: A reliable source of creativity, insight and inspired ideas.

Authenticity: The freedom to be yourself, speak your truth and do what you know to be right.

Intuition: Alignment with your intuition and inner wisdom, your internal guidance system (aka 'wisdom', 'gut feel' or 'common sense').

Presence: Present, aware and available to the moment, connected with your mind, your body and the world around you.

Connection: Warm, genuine connections with other people, leading to stronger relationships with clients, colleagues, friends, family members and lovers.

Clarity: A clear mind, free from contaminated thinking, fully present and in the moment, with the levels of performance, satisfaction and enjoyment that brings.

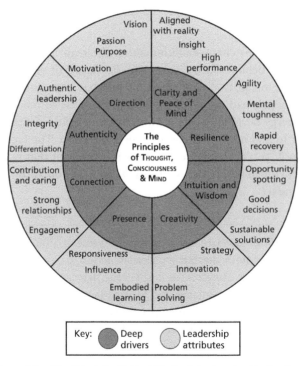

Figure 6.2:   The Principles Behind Clarity Drive Leadership Attributes

Practicality check: How is being a leader going to help me get results?

Being a results-creator *means* being a leader; venturing into the unknown, facing your insecurities and taking risks. It means developing your creative muscles; experimenting, risking failure and braving the fear of criticism.

We started this chapter talking about the realization that the principles behind clarity represent the future of psychology. That one realization captivated me and has been guiding me ever since. It had me sell the business I'd spent so much time and energy developing, walk away from the field I'd become a leader in and move in an entirely new direction. The fact that the book you're reading even *exists* is a result of that realization. So when you have a realization, how do you know what to do next?

Bottom line results: Leadership is a business essential. The qualities of leadership are innate, but good leaders *appear* to be in short supply. Why? While everyone has innate leadership capacities, they're often obscured by contaminated thinking (e.g. fear of failure, of criticism, of the unknown, of responsibility, of public speaking). But as you realize this for yourself, you'll find contaminated thinking being subtracted and your innate leadership capacities emerging.

keep exploring ⁝ connect with others
share your discoveries ⁝ deepen your understanding

Experiment: What are some of the times and situations in your life when you are (or have been) a leader?

www.jamiesmart.com/results6

7

The Liberating
Truth About Goals

Integrity has no need of rules.

Albert Camus, Journalist, author, winner of the
Nobel Prize in Literature, 1957

**'A study of the 1953 graduates of Yale University clearly
demonstrates this point. . .'**

In his bestselling book, *Unlimited Power*, Anthony Robbins
describes a study of the Yale University Class of 1953 and the
follow-up, 20 years later. He explains that the 3% of the class
who had clear written goals and a plan for achieving them were
more financially successful by 1973 than the other 97% of
the class combined. In addition, he reports that the 3% scored
more highly on measures such as happiness and joy. Robbins

uses this study as proof of the power of goal setting, stating that 'the difference in people's abilities to fully tap their personal resources is directly affected by their goals'. There's only one problem with the oft-mentioned *Yale University Goals Study*...

It never actually happened...

Yale University has stated *categorically* that no such study of the class of 1953 ever occurred. The likely explanation appears to be that the 1953 Yale study was such a compelling *story* that many of the world's best-known motivational speakers of the day used it to validate 'success systems' based on audacious goals, unwavering self-belief and massive action.

By the time you've finished this chapter, you'll see goals for what they are, and understand how you can use them in the context of a far more powerful and sophisticated 'success system' you've been benefiting from your whole life.

What is a goal?

A goal is a thought; nothing more. Any feeling you get when you think about a goal is telling you about your THOUGHT-generated perceptual reality in that moment, *not* about the *result* you're imagining. While a goal can be a useful tool (e.g. for helping you set a direction, organize your efforts or coordinate the efforts of a group of people), it has no power in and of itself.

You have an innate capacity for achieving goals

You set and achieve goals every day. Tasks as mundane as brushing your teeth involve complex nested structures of goals, actions and evidence criteria. We employ these structures automatically without even thinking about it consciously. When viewed through the lens of 'goal achievement', making a cup of tea involves having a goal for some purpose, taking some action and meeting some evidence of completion.

Goal	What do you want? (A cup of tea)
Purpose	Why do you want that? (I'm thirsty and want a hot drink)
Evidence criteria	How will you know you've got it? (My thirst will be quenched and I will feel satisfied)
Action	What needs to happen for that to happen? (Make and drink tea)

But if you look at it more closely, the action 'Make and drink tea' is itself composed of a number of goals, each with their own evidence and action (e.g. boil water, put teabag in cup, pour water on teabag, allow tea to brew, add milk, drink tea). If we looked even more closely, each of these would be composed of yet more goals with *their* own evidence and action.

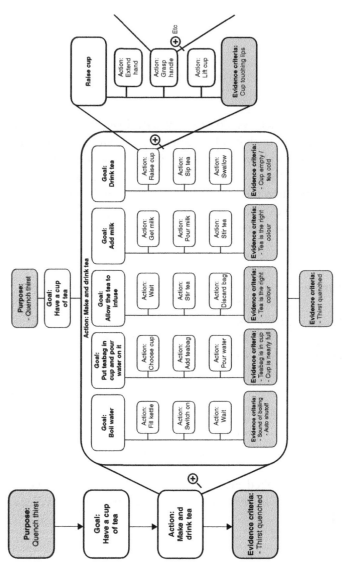

Figure 7.1: Embodied Understanding Drives Results-creation

The capacity that allows you to make a cup of tea without thinking about it is the same capacity that is going to support you in creating the results that matter to you: *embodied understanding*. When we have embodied understanding of a domain, we engage the complex network of relationships that allows us to get *results* in that context.

You have embodied understanding of a domain when you understand it at such a deep level that you don't even have to think about it. Your ability to create results in a given domain is a function of your embodied understanding of the *reality* of that domain. A person who has a deep embodied understanding of driving is likely to be a better driver than someone who's never been behind the wheel. So what does this have to do with the results you want to create? Here's what:

Your ability to create results that are a perfect fit for you and your life is a function of your embodied understanding of how your mind works.

Just as an athlete's embodied understanding of gravity will determine the quality of their athletic results, and a doctor's embodied understanding of anatomy will have an influence on the quality of their interventions. . .

Your understanding of how your mind and perception work have an across-the-board influence on your ability to create the results that matter to you.

You are already a results-creator

We all have places where we're easily able to create the results we want (areas where we're *already* well aligned with reality). And we each have areas where we struggle; areas where we're *not* so well aligned with reality. For example. . .

- The mother who manages to juggle a hectic family schedule, but can't seem to achieve a healthy bodyweight.

- The entrepreneur who makes money easily, but who struggles with their intimate relationships.

- The therapist who has a profound impact on their clients, but lives hand-to-mouth with no stable income.

- The company director who inspires loyalty and hard work in their people, but struggles with addictive behaviours.

- The analyst who's really good at their job, but yearns to do something else and doesn't know what.

Toxic goals

'Toxic goals' are goals grounded in the outside-in misunderstanding. They typically have an 'I'll be happy when. . .' or 'I can't be happy until. . .' structure, for instance. . .

- I'll be successful once I earn a million dollars.

- I can't be happy until I leave this boring job and find work I love.

- I'll feel secure once I'm married.

- I can't feel free until I have a location-independent lifestyle.

- I'll be successful once our share price hits $100.

Toxic goals are based around the false belief that our feelings are giving us information about our (future) circumstances, but that's not possible. Consider this imaginary conversation. . .

Karen: I feel stressed.	*(The feeling of stress is a signal that Karen's in stressful thinking. This is a healthy and useful signal.)*
Bob: Why?	*(Bob innocently invites her to blame something other than THOUGHT in the moment; to step into La-la Land.)*
Karen: I've got too much to do and not enough time to do it in.	*(Karen innocently and mistakenly assigns her feelings to an external factor. She is now in La-la Land.)*
Bob: That sucks. What are you going to do about it?	*(Bob validates her mistake.)*
Karen: Find a job that's not so stressful.	*(Because Karen believes her feelings are coming from an external factor, it makes sense to look to the outside if she wants to change how she feels. This is a recipe for a toxic goal.)*

So am I saying Karen shouldn't find a new job? No. I have no idea whether she should find a new job or not. But here's what I *do* know:

> *When you're looking at the world from a place of*
> *misunderstanding, the goals you come up with will*
> *reflect that misunderstanding.*
> *When you're looking at the world from a place of clarity,*
> *the goals you come up with will reflect that clarity.*

When we drift out of reality and into La-la Land, caught up in contaminated thinking, we lose touch with common sense and wisdom. The moment we fall out of contaminated thinking and into the present moment, the way forward is clear and the next step is obvious. . .

- Sometimes the next step is to press ahead with what we're doing.

- Sometimes the next step is to rest.

- Sometimes the next step is to do something different.

- Sometimes the next step is to wait for inspiration.

Authentic desires

Authentic desires are results you want just because you want them. They may not even make rational sense, but they're authentic expressions of your being. Think about that for a moment. . .

Who you really are is the infinite intelligence and creative potential of life, the formless principles of THOUGHT, CONSCIOUSNESS *and* MIND.
Your authentic desires are an expression of that infinite intelligence and creative potential.
There is an intelligence and wisdom in you and your desires.

Authentic desires often arrive as insights and realizations. Here are some of the questions I sometimes ask my clients to start pointing them in the direction of their authentic desires. . .

- What do you want? What would you like to have happen? What would you love to create or bring into being?

- How will you know you've got that result? What will you see, hear and feel that will let you know you've got it?

- If you could wave a magic wand and have everything the way you want it to be, what would that look like?

- What would you want if you knew you couldn't fail? What would you want if you knew it was OK to fail?

- What would you do if you had £100 million in the bank?

- What would you do if all work paid the same, and you could get whatever work you like?

- What would you want if you knew you were going to be happy, secure, successful and loved, whether you got it or not?

- What would you want if you didn't have to be unhappy about not getting it?

The purpose of these questions *isn't* for you to come up with specific goals as answers to them (though that may happen); the purpose is to guide you into a reflective space where you're more likely to have insights and realizations about what's important and meaningful to you and for you.

When is it useful to set goals?

Set goals when it makes sense. If it makes sense to set a specific target, set one. If it doesn't, don't. As stated earlier, goals can be useful for helping you set a direction, organize your own efforts or coordinate the efforts of a group of people. If you're creating a complex result that involves the work of many people, or things happening in a particular sequence, goals can be an incredibly useful part of the planning process (if you're building a house, you probably don't want the decorators arriving to start painting before the walls are up). But goals have no power in and of themselves.

Practicality check: How is having a better understanding of goals going to help me get results?

In Chapter 1, I introduced you to *The Clarity Results Model, Clarity plus Action equals Results*. Goals can be useful *tools* for prioritizing, co-ordinating and directing a variety of *actions*. The better you understand the tool (how you can use it, when to use it, when not to use it, etc), the more creative you can be with it.

CLARITY   plus   **ACTION**   equals   **RESULTS**

Figure 7.2: The CLARITY® Results Model

So once you've got clarity about a result you want to create, how do you get into action?

Bottom line results: Most organizations rely on goals, targets and objectives to organize their efforts. This is a practical matter. But as soon as people believe their *psychological safety* is dependent on hitting the goal, they're at risk of creating a contaminated culture of stress, anxiety and unsustainable pressure. Of course, some goals are extremely important and can influence the very survival of an organization. The more you're able to approach goals from a place of clarity and common sense, the more likely you are to prevail.

keep exploring ⁘ connect with others
share your discoveries ⁘ deepen your understanding

Experiment: What are some of the results you'd love to create? You might like to take a few minutes to read the questions posed earlier in this chapter, and maybe even write down what occurs to you.

www.jamiesmart.com/results7

8

Moving from Resistance to Action

....

Action expresses priorities.

Mahatma Gandhi, Lawyer, politician

'I'm scared. . . I'm not sure I want to go on the ride. . .'

My daughter Tallulah and I were standing in line; it was going to be her first time on a roller-coaster. Tallulah and I had been looking forward to this day for years, but as we stood in the queue, she was gripped by anxiety and having second thoughts. In the end, her desire for adventure won out. The next two minutes were intoxicating as we dived, looped and swooped through the park, reaching speeds of 75 kilometres per hour. Tallulah loved it! When the ride was over, she said,

'I was really frightened in the queue, but the ride was amazing! I really enjoyed it'. Her statement stopped me in my tracks, and I asked her what she made of that. She said, 'I guess I was feeling my thinking in the queue, but I thought I was feeling the roller-coaster'.

Tallulah had seen through the oldest trick in the book, the mistaken belief that we're feeling something *other than* THOUGHT in the moment. We're always living in the feeling of the principle of THOUGHT, taking form in the moment. But it often *seems* as though we're feeling something *other than* THOUGHT. Why? Because THOUGHT points the finger at anything but itself. When she was in the queue, it seemed as though Tallulah's feelings were coming from her future roller-coaster ride. In fact, she was experiencing a THOUGHT-generated illusion in the present. I told her, 'As you go through life, you will see countless examples of people who believe they're feeling the roller-coaster of their future, when really they're standing in the queue, feeling THOUGHT in the moment'.

So what does this have to do with motivation, action and momentum? Here's what:

You don't need to feel motivated to take action.

In fact, it turns out that the most relevant time to take action can often be when you're *not* feeling motivated, enthusiastic or inspired. By the time you've finished this chapter, you're going to understand how to make progress on any project, no matter how motivated or unmotivated you feel, and no matter how uncomfortable or resistant you may have been with it until now.

DISTINCTION: The inspiration myth vs the perspiration reality

The inventor Thomas Edison famously described genius as 'one percent inspiration, ninety-nine percent perspiration'. The **inspiration myth** goes something like this: 'I'll start taking action *once* I'm feeling inspired.'

The problem with the inspiration myth is that it can keep people stuck in passivity, waiting for metaphorical lightning to strike so they can start moving forward.

While acts of creation *sometimes* result from this kind of inspiration, it's the exception rather than the rule. A much more common and reliable pattern of creation is the **perspiration reality**: 'I'm not feeling inspired, but I'll start taking action anyway.'

Many of my clients appreciate *The Clarity Productivity Quadrant*:

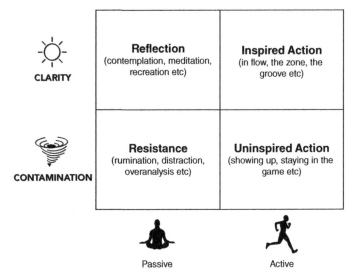

Figure 8.1:   The CLARITY® Productivity Quadrant

The quadrant describes four zones:

1.   The Zone of Resistance (*passive*)

We all oscillate between periods of clarity and times when we get caught up in our thinking. When we're caught up, it's almost always an example of contaminated thinking, the mistaken belief that our feelings are coming from somewhere *other than* THOUGHT in the moment. The *Zone of Resistance* isn't much fun. Nevertheless, we all end up there from time to time. We're not all 100% productive 100% of the time. You might like to reflect on the question, 'Where do I believe my experience is coming from?' When we're in the *Zone of Resistance*, it almost always seems like our feelings are letting us know about the future, the past, our circumstances, other people or ourselves. Alternatively, you can jump into *uninspired* action.

2. The Zone of Uninspired Action (*active*)

The *Zone of Uninspired Action* often accounts for the 'perspiration reality' we explored earlier. Getting into action gives you something to be doing and focusing on. Your mind is a self-correcting system, so you're going to get fresh new thinking/feeling eventually. When you're taking action, it's surprising how often new thinking shows up. When a person's in the *Zone of Uninspired Action*, there's sometimes a sense of strain, struggle and 'slogging away at it'. That's OK; as my dear friend and colleague Garret Kramer says, 'Stay in the game.' You may even find yourself pausing and easing into a *reflective* state of mind.

3. The Zone of Reflection (*passive*)

The *Zone of Reflection* is a powerful source of fresh new thinking, a zone of renewal and regeneration. Newton's theory of universal gravitation, Archimedes' eureka moment and Steve Jobs' insights about the future of the music business all came in moments of reflection, when they weren't actively thinking about the matter at hand. There are countless contexts where people enter a reflective and contemplative state of mind (e.g. walking, sitting by the ocean, riding, meditating, reading, listening to certain music, sitting in the bath). As you get a deeper understanding of the principles behind clarity, you'll find yourself being guided into the *Zone of Reflection* more easily and spontaneously. And from time to time, you'll get struck with inspiration, an insight that shows you the way forward. When that happens, it's time for *inspired* action.

4. The Zone of Inspired Action (*active*)

The *Zone of Inspired Action* is where you can't seem to put a foot wrong; where everything's falling into place and you feel guided and directed. Enjoy it when it comes, and stay in the game when it doesn't. Even when it's nowhere to be found, you can relax in the knowledge that it's only ever a thought away.

The art of making things happen

Do something. . .

> *When you take action, you can discover things that you're unlikely to stumble upon in the privacy of your own head. . . You put your theories and ideas about life to the test, and get direct feedback from an impartial agent: reality!*

As you get a deeper understanding of the principles behind clarity, you'll find yourself with a stronger foundation for the action you take. You'll become more attuned to your own rhythms, knowing when to act and when to pause for reflection. As you keep waking up to the power of wisdom and intuition, you'll come to rely more and more on them as a source of insight, guidance and realization.

CLARITY   plus   **ACTION**   equals   **RESULTS**

Figure 8.2:   The CLARITY® Results Model

Practicality check: How is moving from resistance to action going to help me get results?

As your understanding of subtractive psychology continues to deepen, you'll find that you have a stronger foundation for the action you take. When you take action, you put your theories and ideas about life to the test. You get direct feedback from an impartial agent: reality!

So as your personal transformation continues, it's time to jump into your *interpersonal* transformation, a domain that will give you plenty of opportunity for connection, experimentation and action.

Bottom line results: In a world awash with 'productivity systems', it can be a relief to realize that you possess a *built-in* productivity system that is tailor-made for you, and the situations you find yourself in. As you get more in tune with your own rhythms, and continue deepening your understanding of these principles, you'll find this having an enormous impact on your ability to create results.

---

keep exploring ⁘ connect with others
share your discoveries ⁘ deepen your understanding

Experiment: Is there something you've been struggling to bring into being until now? Perhaps it's something you'd love to make happen, but you don't know where to start. What's a next step you could take? Just for fun, make a start, just to see what happens. . .

www.jamiesmart.com/results8

PART TWO

IMPACT
Your Interpersonal
Transformation

Everything about us – our brains, our minds and our bodies – is geared towards collaboration in social systems. This is our most powerful survival strategy, the key to our success as a species, and it is precisely this that breaks down in most forms of mental suffering.

Bessel van der Kolk
Psychiatrist, PTSD researcher

We cannot live for ourselves alone. Our lives are connected by a thousand invisible threads, and along these sympathetic bers, our actions run as causes and return to us as results.

Herman Melville
Novelist, teacher, sailor, poet

9

The Principles of Impact

....

Everyone needs a coach.

Bill Gates, Co-founder of Microsoft,
entrepreneur, philanthropist

'Would you like me to collaborate with you on growing your business?'

Pete Bryceland responded to my message minutes after I'd sent it. 'Yes I would!' He'd been finding it challenging to make a living as a coach (he'd earned less than £20,000 that year). He wanted to earn significantly more money, enjoy the process more and feel greater freedom. Pete loved coaching, and got great results with his clients, but found charging by the hour frustrating and difficult. He wanted to have more committed clients, increase his income and stabilize his cash flow.

But there was a problem: Pete hated selling.

Pete joined the beta-test group for a new programme I was developing, and I ended up coaching him in front of a live audience a few weeks later. He explained that when he had conversations with potential clients, they were excited about working with him, but as soon as they started asking about what it would cost, Pete became awkward, disconnected and tongue-tied. He'd lost three prospective clients in the previous few weeks due to this 'selling-anxiety'. As we talked, Pete started becoming more reflective, and a sense of connection started developing between us. About 20 minutes into the conversation, Pete had a realization, and started to see the situation differently. He got in touch with me a month later to let me know that he'd signed up two clients on packages of £10,000 each since our coaching conversation. He'd made more money as a result of that one insight than he had in the previous year!

Many of the greatest performers on the planet have coaches. From golfer Rory McIlroy to Google CEO Eric Schmidt; from pop diva Beyoncé to surgeon Atul Gawande. Why? Because the perspective, understanding and mindset of an impactful coach can unlock your potential and bring out your best performance, calling forth extraordinary transformations and results.

And what does this have to do with the principles of impact?

It turns out that you can realize the leverage points the world's most transformational coaches use to create massive impact – in your own life and in the lives of others. You see, the principles of impact apply in *every situation*, whether you're giving a speech or out on a first date, whether you're parenting your teenager or applying for a job.

The Clarity Impact Model

You know those days when everything falls into place, you get the ideas you need exactly when you need them, and you finish the day feeling productive and fulfilled? And then there are those *other* days, when it really seems like you would have been better just to *stay* in bed. The days when everything seems like a chore, and it's tough to find your groove. The difference between those two days is the state of mind you're in. . . your level of clarity. Your level of clarity determines how you're showing up in the world, and the impact you're going to have. *The Clarity Impact Model* is a simple way of relating to your innate capacity for learning, changing, growing, communicating and getting results. It applies equally to individuals, 1:1 relationships and groups. You can think of it as a metaphor that points to the principles behind clarity and your innate capacity for having an impact. It consists of the following elements:

1   Clarity of connection

2   Clarity of thought

3   Clarity of understanding

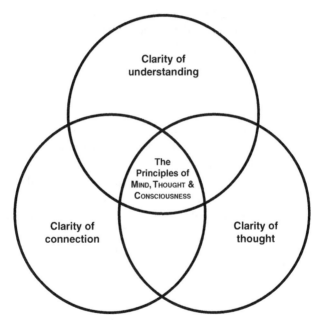

Figure 9.1:   The CLARITY® Impact Model

You're going to get an overview of these three kinds of clarity in this chapter, then we'll be exploring each of them more deeply in the chapters that follow.

1. Clarity of connection

Social groups are a big part of the reality we're built for. The feeling of connection can be a powerful communicator of trust and credibility when it comes to persuasion, influence and leadership. In more intimate relationships, the feeling of love and connection is the rich soil that feeds the roots of the relationship and allows it to grow and evolve. We all have times when we're feeling connected (to another person, to our true selves, to life as a whole). We also have times when we feel less connected, or even isolated. When you're feeling connected, there's a sense of closeness and intimacy that carries its own credibility. When we're hanging out in La-la Land, caught up in contaminated thinking, we lose that sense of connection. The moment you fall out of contaminated thinking and into the reality of the moment, your sense of connection re-emerges.

2. Clarity of thought

Clarity of thought is a predictor of high performance, valuable insights and impactful communications. Unsurprisingly, clarity of thought is also correlated with a deeper sense of connection. We all have times when we're clear-headed, present and available to the moment. We also have times when we're preoccupied, with a lot on our minds. Clarity of thought is the variable that determines where on that spectrum you're showing up. When we're caught up in contaminated thinking, our clarity of thought is low. The moment you wake up from the outside-in misunderstanding, clarity of thought returns.

3.　Clarity of understanding

Everyone has their own understanding of how life works. In some areas of life, your embodied understanding is closely aligned with reality, and you get good results. In other areas, your embodied understanding is adrift from reality, and you struggle. The greater your awareness of the inside-out nature of the mind, the greater your clarity of understanding is. Your clarity of understanding is the ultimate leverage point for increasing the amount of time you spend clear-headed and feeling connected. When you *do* get caught up in contaminated thinking, your clarity of understanding determines how quickly your mind will self-correct.

The principles of impact

The Clarity Impact Model is relevant in any domain that involves people (e.g. leadership, coaching, parenting, teaching, public speaking, influence, relationships etc). The reason this model applies across all contexts is simple. . .

> *The principles behind clarity are at play in every human interaction. . .*
> *If a person is having an experience, it's being created by the principles of* MIND, THOUGHT *and* CONSCIOUSNESS.

It's liberating to realize that *you're already connected* to the principles of impact. The principles of MIND, THOUGHT and

THE PRINCIPLES OF IMPACT

Consciousness are creating your experience *right now*, in this very moment. As you deepen your understanding of the nature of these principles, you'll increase your ability to have an impact with others and create meaningful results.

Practicality check: How are the principles of impact going to help me get results?

- You've *already* been using the principles of impact to get the results you've created so far in your life, whether you've realized it or not.

- A deeper understanding of subtractive psychology will help you experience a clear mind and deeper connections more frequently.

- As you learn to navigate using these principles, you'll start experiencing the inevitable results of becoming more closely aligned with reality, including richer relationships, effortless influence and increased creativity.

Transformational results

I conducted a case-study interview with Pete Bryceland a year after he joined my programme to document what the impact of this understanding had been for him. Pete's results have been transformational. He now feels a sense of ease and enjoyment about money and enrolling clients. Pete coaches business owners, executives and managers who are feeling overwhelmed and under constant pressure to perform. He says, 'If I want more money, I just go out and get it.' He's increased his income significantly, but he said the *biggest* impact has been the sense of freedom and security he now feels. This has meant he's been able to spend more time with his family (one of the main reasons he decided to set up his own business in the first place).

My transformational conversation with Pete started with a deep sense of connection. So how can you start experiencing that kind of connection to help you create the results that matter to you?

Bottom line results: Every business relies on people – colleagues, clients, stakeholders, suppliers – to get results. *The Clarity Impact Model* explains how the principles behind clarity play out in every human situation. As you experiment with these principles, you're going to find yourself enjoying your interactions more, and having a more positive effect on others, with predictably positive results.

| CLARITY | plus | ACTION | equals | RESULTS |

Figure 9.2:   The CLARITY® Results Model

__keep exploring ⁜ connect with others__
__share your discoveries ⁜ deepen your understanding__

Experiment: What are some of the places and situations in your life where you're *already* having an impact? Reflect on the effect your state of mind has been having either to constrain or amplify your impact.

www.jamiesmart.com/results9

10

The Secret of Powerful Connection

No man is an island, entire of itself; every man is a piece of the continent.

John Donne, Poet, priest, lawyer

'I knew I shouldn't have come here. I'm booking a flight home. . .'

My girlfriend and I had arrived in Hawaii the night before, and she'd been intoxicated by the beautiful scents, warm breeze and tropical vibe. We'd been feeling close and connected, but the next morning she was cold, panicked and distant. She said, 'I'm booking a flight home.'

I could see what was going on. Her feelings were letting her know about THOUGHT in the moment, but she mistakenly believed they were letting her know about Hawaii and me. She said, 'I knew this was a mistake. Why did I listen to you?' Now I was starting to get annoyed. *What was I doing here with this moody woman? I hope she does get a flight home so I can relax and enjoy this exotic corner of paradise.* And that's when the voice of wisdom whispered in my ear. . .

'Where do you believe your feelings are coming from? Do you think they're letting you know about her?'

The realization hit me in a flash. I'd been doing *exactly* the same thing *she* was. My girlfriend had been blaming her feelings on Hawaii; I'd been blaming my feelings on my girlfriend. Peace, humility and connection came rushing back to me as I fell out of contaminated thinking and into the moment. I'd fallen out of the illusion of separation and landed in the fact of connection. You see. . .

You're always connected, to everything and everyone. . .
Whether you realize it or not. . .

My heart went out to her. My position of judgement and justified anger had been replaced with love and compassion. I didn't say anything, but I could see her innocence in the face of the outside-in misunderstanding. A moment later, she fell out of it too. 'Don't mind me, I'm just being silly.' The storm which had been threatening to destroy our holiday had passed, and the sunshine of clarity and connection had emerged.

We all live and work in a matrix of relationships, and in one way or another, many of our results are reliant on other people. As technology makes our world more tangibly connected, social and emotional intelligence are becoming more important than ever. By the time you've finished this chapter, you'll understand where the experience of connection comes from, what gets in the way of it, and how to experience effortless connection more of the time, in the situations where it matters.

Where does connection come from?

We've each had the experience (even if only occasionally) of feeling deeply connected with ourselves, with another person and even with life itself. And everyone's had the experience (even if only occasionally) of feeling isolated, disconnected and alone. Both of these polarities are universal aspects of the human experience, and an understanding of them is incredibly powerful when it comes to relationships. To understand where connection comes from, we're going to be drawing a distinction between the *experience* of connection and the *fact* of connection:

DISTINCTION: The fact of connection vs the experience of connection

We are all made of the same formless energy. Like waves in an ocean, we are all part of the same undivided wholeness. Just as waves don't leave the ocean and 'go solo', we are never disconnected from this infinite ocean of energy. This is **the fact of connection**.

The experience of connection is often described as a feeling of love and closeness combined with rapport. People sometimes say, 'We just clicked' or describe themselves as being on the same wavelength.

The felt <u>experience</u> of connection is an expression of the <u>fact</u> of connection. . .
You become aware of it when there's nothing getting in the way.

The thing that tends to *get* in the way is contaminated thinking arising from the outside-in misunderstanding. The experience of connection rapidly evaporates when we lose ourselves in contaminated thinking. But the moment we insightfully see the inside-out nature of life, we fall out of our contaminated thinking and wake up to reality. As we return to the present moment, we find ourselves back in the experience of connection with our true nature, with other people, and with life as a whole.

Connection is the 'transformation superhighway' when it comes to impact.

The experience of connection is natural when there's nothing else in the way. But **the fact of connection** is constant, even when you're not aware of it. And here's the great thing: as you insightfully realize connection as a pre-existing *fact*, the *experience* of connection becomes deeper and more frequent.

IMPLICATION: Separate realities

We each live in a separate, THOUGHT-generated perceptual reality. Your feelings are giving you feedback about the 'glasses' you're wearing, not who or what you're looking at. How you perceive other people is always consistent with *your own* level of clarity in the moment. . .

- When you're feeling frustrated or angry, other people often appear to be the source of that frustration or anger.

- When you're feeling loving and appreciative, other people may appear to be a source of blessings.

The Clarity Relationship Quadrant provides a simple way of understanding this. . .

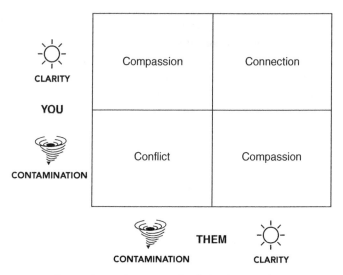

Figure 10.1: The CLARITY® Relationship Quadrant

1. The zone of conflict

Bob and Jane feel angry at each other. Their angry feelings are letting each of them know they're 'wearing angry-goggles', but each of them *mistakenly* believes their feelings are telling them about the other person. They're in *The Zone of Conflict*.

2. The zone of connection

Bob and Jane have a big shouting match, followed by passionate make-up sex. In the heat of the moment, their heads clear, and they start feeling deeply connected to each other.

3. The zone of compassion (1)

Later on, Bob starts getting upset again, but Jane still feels connected and clear-headed. She sees that Bob has just lost his bearings, and her heart goes out to him, full of compassion.

4. The zone of compassion (2)

The next day, Bob wakes up with a clear head. He goes to Jane to apologize for his hasty words the night before, but she's in a rush to get out the door and snaps at him. He sees that Jane has lost her bearings. He feels compassion for her, seeing the innocence in the ebb and flow of her thinking.

The Clarity Relationship Quadrant works on the basis that:

- Your feelings are always letting you know about THOUGHT taking form in your experience, moment to moment.

- Other people will appear to be consistent with *your* THOUGHT-generated perceptual reality.

- When neither participant has clarity, it's a recipe for conflict.

- When *one* person in a relationship has clarity, it creates space for the other person to start finding clarity too.

This is incredibly encouraging news; it means that clarity in your relationships starts with you.

Practicality check: How is connection going to help me get results?

- When people feel connected to you, they experience you as honest, authentic and transparent.

- When you're feeling connected to your true self and to life, you're more open to insights, realizations and innovative thinking.

- When it comes to impacting another person, the feeling of connection creates a space where genuine communication can take place, and transformation can occur.

So how can you learn to rely on that clarity emerging when and where you need it?

Bottom line results: One of the simplest ways to get the benefits of connection is by listening deeply to the person or people you're with. Listening and connection can turn a previously unproductive meeting into a source of fresh new insights and innovative solutions, deepening relationships in the process.

***keep exploring ❖ connect with others
share your discoveries ❖ deepen your understanding***

Experiment: In your conversations, notice the ebb and flow of the feeling of connection. If you want to increase the sense of connection, listen with 'nothing on your mind'. When you truly listen, you allow yourself to be present to the other person, bathing them in your attention.

www.jamiesmart.com/results10

11

The Source of Superb Performance

....

I saw the angel in the marble and carved until I set him free.

Michelangelo, Sculptor, painter, architect

'If you think too much about a race you just make yourself more nervous. . .'

Olympic Gold medal-winner Usain Bolt is currently the world's fastest sprinter. Before the race, while his competitors are running through complex pre-race rituals, Bolt fools around and chats with the crowd. When asked why, he said, 'I've learned over the years that if you think too much about a race you just make yourself more nervous.' Bolt understands that wherever you're headed, clarity is your best ally for helping you get there. So why is it that some people produce world-class performances over and over again, while others struggle when the heat is on?

High performance leads to superb results

People give their best performances when they've got nothing on their mind. When your mind is clear, you're available to the moment, connected to your innate source of guidance, resilience and creativity. And where does high performance come from? Your state of mind.

How your state of mind affects your performance

In their December 2014 *Harvard Business Review* article, 'How Your State of Mind Affects Your Performance', researchers Caillet, Hirshberg and Petti reported their findings from a survey of 740 leaders internationally. 94% of the leaders identified the states that drove the highest levels of performance as 'calm', 'happy' and 'energized' (CHE). At the other end of the spectrum, leaders admitted to spending a certain amount of time in low-performance states; 'frustrated', 'anxious', 'tired' and 'stressed' (FATS). The article suggested that CHE states not only drove high performance; these states also seemed to be 'transmitted' to other people. Conversely, the FATS states often delivered *short-term* results, but were damaging in the long term, particularly in the domain of relationships.

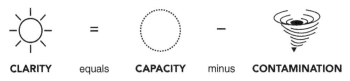

CLARITY   equals   **CAPACITY**   minus   **CONTAMINATION**

Figure 11.1:   The CLARITY® Equation

When we struggle with FATS states, we've been hijacked by contaminated thinking. The CHE states, on the other hand, are natural for us when our minds are *free* from contaminated thinking.

State control: correlation does not imply causation

Caillet, Hirshberg and Petti then ask, 'How do leaders shift from lower states of mind to higher states of mind and improve their effectiveness and performance?' As you'll understand, this question invites leaders to look *away* from the mind's self-clearing capacity, and *misattribute* the power to things in the (neutral) world of form.

Unsurprisingly, the executives identified a variety of additive approaches, including visualization, positive thinking, deep breathing, listening to music, exercise, a healthy diet and adequate sleep. While it would be foolish to argue against the value of exercise, a healthy diet or adequate sleep, this is a classic case of confusing *correlation* with *causation*. A person's thoughts, states, words and behaviour are consistent with their level of consciousness/clarity of understanding. A person who's operating at a higher level of consciousness will tend to spend more time in CHE states, and make healthier choices in general. While there can certainly be the appearance of a 'virtuous circle' quality in this, the idea that the states are caused by (or hampered by) external factors is fundamentally untrue. So if methods, techniques and practices are not the answer, what is?

The only thing you need for a high-performance state of mind

Think of one of your favourite films or TV shows. There are two things you need to enjoy the show:

You have to be able to be 'swept away' by the film

The best directors are masters of creating an illusionary reality. They use sound and light to create an *imaginary* world; a La-la Land. When we get 'swept away' by a movie, we get drawn into the director's illusionary world and experience it as real. We temporarily 'forget' that the characters and events we're experiencing are light and shadows on a screen and relate to them as though they're really happening. When someone *doesn't* get swept away by a film, you'll hear them say something like, 'I couldn't get into it.' They weren't 'fooled' by the illusionary reality, so couldn't suspend their disbelief and enter into the director's La-la Land.

You have to be able to 'wake up' from the film's illusionary reality

While it's wonderful to be swept away by a film, we also have to be able to wake up to the fact that it's an illusion (otherwise you'd phone the fire department if flames appeared on the screen). Our ability to fall out of the director's La-la Land is a function of our understanding of the *nature* of movies. You developed this understanding at an early age and today, your ability to 'wake up' from the film is automatic. Of course, little children don't yet understand the nature of film. Telling a child who doesn't understand the nature of film that 'it's just a movie' has no effect. It's your embodied understanding that allows you to wake up from the illusion and return to reality. Of course, you never actually left reality; you just *thought* you did.

Enjoying a movie requires an oscillation between these two positions; being swept away by the film's illusionary reality, occasionally punctuated by waking up to the fact that it's just a movie. This is exactly the same kind of oscillation you need to enjoy your life, to wake up from FATS and experience CHE states of mind, more and more of the time.

You have to be able to be 'swept away' by the principle of THOUGHT

The principle of THOUGHT is the best film director in the world. It creates a multi-sensory illusionary reality that we bring to life using the principle of CONSCIOUSNESS and experience as real. When we're moved by the sight of a beautiful sunrise, filled up with love for someone we care about or inspired by a leader's visionary words, we've been swept away by the principle of THOUGHT. Those *beautiful* feelings are coming from THOUGHT taking form in the moment within you, but it often *seems* like they're coming from the sunrise, the leader or the loved one. When we're anxious about a future appointment, worried about someone we care about or angry about someone's past behaviours, we've been swept away by the principle of THOUGHT. Those *uncomfortable* feelings are coming from THOUGHT taking form in the moment, but it *seems* like they're coming from somewhere *other than* THOUGHT; from the appointment, the person we're concerned about or the wrong-doer's behaviours. This is the illusionary power of THOUGHT.

You have to be able to 'wake up' from THOUGHT's illusory reality

We all get swept away by THOUGHT, but we all have the power to wake up from THOUGHT's illusory reality; to fall out of the La-la Land of our contaminated thinking, and fall present to the moment. We've all had the experience of being very worried about something before going to sleep, then waking up the next morning wondering how we'd managed to get so bothered about it. Little children intuitively grasp the illusory nature of THOUGHT, able to flit from sobbing with misery to giggling with joy in the blink of an eye. In any moment, we can *realize* that we're feeling THOUGHT taking form, and *not* what we're thinking about. The instant this happens, we fall out of the La-la Land of our misunderstanding, and 'fall awake' to the present.

A rich, enjoyable experience of life relies on an oscillation between the two positions mentioned above; getting swept away by the principle of THOUGHT in the moment, then waking up to the illusory nature of THOUGHT. And as you continue to explore the principles behind clarity, your understanding of the deceptive and illusory nature of THOUGHT will allow you to enjoy this oscillation more and more. And it turns out that's the only thing you need to live a life you love and experience high-performance states of mind more of the time.

> *The one thing you need to enjoy a movie is an*
> *understanding of the nature of film.*
> *The one thing you need to enjoy your life is an*
> *understanding of the nature of THOUGHT.*

And remember; you're *built* for reality; you're optimized for results. The CLARITY® model is a *subtractive* psychology; as your understanding of these principles continues to deepen, it takes things *off* your mind, giving you *less* to think about.

Practicality check: How is a clear mind going to help me get results?

People get their best ideas and deliver their best performances when they've got nothing on their mind. As you translate insights into action, you create results.

| CLARITY | plus | ACTION | equals | RESULTS |

Figure 11.2:   The CLARITY® Results Model

We started this chapter with Usain Bolt explaining how he avoids overthinking prior to a race. He went on to say, 'My mind automatically turns on to what I have got to do when I need it to.'

So what enables a person to have such a high level of confidence in and reliance on the mind's self-clearing ability, and all the other innate capacities for creating results?

Bottom line results: Clarity of understanding supports the 'high-performance' states of mind which drive results. Both high-performance and low-performance states of mind are highly contagious. Act accordingly.

keep exploring ❖ connect with others
share your discoveries ❖ deepen your understanding

Experiment: Sports commentators will almost always attribute performances (good and bad) to external factors. Competitors will often attribute *poor* performances to external factors. But when they're playing *well*, notice how their explanations change. What are some of the times or situations when you perform at your best?

www.jamiesmart.com/results11

12

The Catalyst for Transformational Results

....

The difficulty's not getting new ideas; new ideas are cheap. I mean there are plenty of new ideas. It's getting rid of the old ideas; that's the hard part.

Carlo Rovelli, Physicist, author

'How are you going to prepare? What plans have you made?'

Ankush Jain (one of my apprentices) was due to be observing during a three-day coaching intensive with a new client, and he wanted to know my plans for the session. The intensive is an in-depth, one-to-one experience designed to transform the client's 'mental and emotional lifestyle' and help them create the results that matter to them. We'd already had two phone calls with Ani (the client) to get clear on what a successful outcome would be from his perspective, so I reminded Ankush of this. 'I know,' he said, 'but you're going to be working with Ani for three days! What plans have you made?' I explained that my plan involved three elements. . .

1 **Calibration**: getting in tune with the client, finding out where they're at and 'getting' their world;

2 **Connection**: finding your way into a feeling of connection with them (and vice versa); and

3 **Education**: allowing yourself to be guided by wisdom and insight about how to share the principles behind clarity with them.

I told him that my primary goal with a client is to create a space where they can have an increase in their clarity of understanding of how their mind *already* works; a jump in consciousness that will give them what they need in order to solve their problems and create the results that matter to them. I explained, 'In any domain, your embodied understanding of how life *already works* is going to make the difference between freedom and frustration, between struggle and success.' I told him. . .

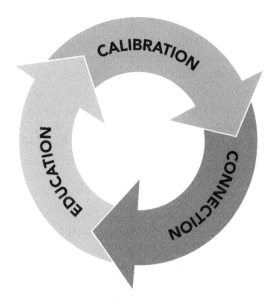

Figure 12.1: The CLARITY® Calibration Model

Your embodied understanding of the mind is the
ultimate leverage point for creating meaningful
results, and living a life you love.

Ankush was convinced there had to be more to it than that.
The client was an entrepreneur who'd bought a company and
managed to double its turnover and profitability in just two
years. But Ani's business success had come at a high price.

He'd been working 16-hour days, and almost never took a day off. He was feeling stressed, pressured and worried about the future. During the first morning of our coaching intensive, I asked him, 'What's your explanation of the cause of your feelings?' Ani wrote an exhaustive list of causes on the whiteboard (including business, money, future, past, staff, and his own personality). Once he'd finished, I asked, 'Would you like to hear *my* explanation for your high levels of stress?' I wrote on the whiteboard, '100% of your feelings are an experience of THOUGHT in the moment'. . .

Ani told me he'd have to reflect on that, so we paused for lunch. When we resumed, he walked up to the whiteboard and put a huge X through his list of 'causes' and said, 'I get it. I've been doing it to myself. I've been feeling my own thinking and *believing* I was feeling my list of circumstances! I don't have a stress problem any more. What are we going to do with the rest of the three days?'

Ankush's jaw nearly hit the floor. . .

Misunderstanding complexifies; understanding simplifies

An 1817 issue of the *New England Journal of Medicine* included an article about childbed fever, a hideous infection which devastated 25% of the women who gave birth in hospitals during the eighteenth and nineteenth centuries. The article identified causes ranging from constipation and vigorous exercise to long journeys and the weather.

The list of spurious causes was accompanied by a list of spurious preventative measures, including avoiding exercise, inducing vomiting and bloodletting. The one true cause (bacteria) and the appropriate preventative measures (antiseptic procedures) were missing. Why? Because the role of germs in causing illness was not understood. Doctors of the day routinely carried out autopsies then conducted internal examinations on pregnant women without first washing their hands.

Throughout history, people have created theories, stories and myths to explain things they don't understand.

When true causes are not understood, spurious causes and solutions proliferate.
Misunderstanding complexifies; understanding simplifies.

The moment we believe our experience is coming from something *other than* THOUGHT in the moment, our heads fill up with bogus causes and potential (equally bogus) solutions. The moment we realize the true source of our experience, our heads clear, and we return to the moment.

The fewer assumptions the better

In every scientific field, the discovery of principles – fundamental laws of nature – is a momentous occurrence that eliminates assumption-rich explanations in favour of simplicity, accuracy and clarity. A principle meets the following three criteria (with thanks to single-paradigm pioneers, Keith Blevens and Valda Monroe):

1 **Constant:** A principle is always true; it never varies.

2 **Explanatory:** A principle provides a complete accounting for how something works; there are no anomalies.

3 **Predictive:** Given the principle, one can predict outcomes in advance.

When we don't understand the *principles* behind an aspect of life, we innocently generate *spurious explanations* for it. The evolution of human knowledge has been driven by the *realization* of explanatory principles that dissolved a plethora of competing theories and bogus explanations.

Psychology is currently in its pre-paradigm phase

The field of psychology is currently awash with multiple incomplete theories, models and bogus explanations. There are literally hundreds of schools of 'talk therapy', each identifying its own 'causes' of struggle (e.g. trauma, loss, neglect) and the 'treatments' necessary to restore a person to full health (e.g. psychoanalysis, cognitive behavioural therapy, electroconvulsive therapy). The same goes for the domain of personal development, leadership development and organizational psychology. The principles behind clarity represent a *paradigm* for psychology: constant, explanatory and predictive.

The ultimate leverage point

Later, Ankush had a sudden and profound insight, saying, 'I know why you didn't have a detailed plan for what you were going to do with the client. His only problem was a *misunderstanding* about where his experience was coming from. All he needed was a realization about how the mind already works, and he'd have the answers he needed.'

An increase in your clarity of understanding is the ultimate leverage point when it comes to creating results. This is the aim of *The Clarity Impact Model*: an increase in your embodied understanding of the principles behind clarity that brings you the direction, inspiration and creativity to create the results that matter to you.

What we did with the rest of the three days

During the remainder of our time together, we looked at Ani's business from this new perspective. One of his issues had been frustration over telling his staff the same thing, over and over again. But when viewed through the lens of *The Clarity Impact Model*, he realized something essential: his staff had been picking up on his stressed-out state of mind *before* he had the chance to say anything. He recognized that nobody does their best listening (or communicating) when they're feeling tense. He discovered that he'd been *accidentally* creating the conditions that found him frustrated and having to repeat himself. During our session, he discovered the power of connection and reawakened his ability to listen deeply to people.

When he returned to work, Ani said that it was almost as though his staff had changed in his absence. They listened to him, and took his suggestions on board. He started spending time with his wife and young son (in fact, on the Friday after our intensive, he left work at 5pm for the first time in two years). When I followed up with Ani several years later, he told me, 'A lot of the battles I'd been fighting in my mind about potential consequences and fear of the unknown just fell away. Having a clear mind allows me to acknowledge the reality of a situation while staying focused on our strengths and open to insight. Clarity and peace of mind have a calming effect on my team *and* my customers, so we're achieving more as a result.'

Ankush has also experienced a profound transformation. At the time of the intensive, he was enjoying a successful career working for a Global 500 company, but he was passionate about becoming a coach. He started using his understanding of the principles behind clarity to deliver additional value to his employer, while developing his impact as a transformation professional. As Ankush cultivated his entrepreneurial instincts and learned about the 'business' of transformation, his client base grew. At the end of 2014, he intuitively knew that the time was right, so he handed in his notice. Today, Ankush is a successful *Clarity Coach* and a leader in the coaching community. He has spoken at conferences in the USA and Europe, and works with clients from around the world, helping them achieve extraordinary results.

Practicality check: How is a jump in consciousness going to help me get results?

When we lose sight of the constant, 100% nature of the thought–feeling connection, our heads fill up with spurious explanations and dubious tactics to resolve them. The moment we wake up to the truth of the principled nature of our experience, the false explanations fall away, and the path forward becomes clear.

So if we're already built for reality, what stops us making progress? If children are born with an intuitive understanding of these principles, why do so many people struggle to create the results that matter to them?

Bottom line results: 'What's the number one result that you perceive would have the biggest positive impact in your business?' While there may well be important operational issues to address, an increase in your clarity of understanding is the *ultimate leverage point* for creating meaningful, sustainable results. Your *embodied understanding* of the inside-out nature of the mind has an 'across the board' impact on your work, and on your life in general.

keep exploring ⁙ connect with others
share your discoveries ⁙ deepen your understanding

Experiment: What are some of the insights and realizations you've already had over the years that are still making a big difference in your life today? As you reflect on some of your more pivotal discoveries, you may begin to notice an increasing appreciation for the value of an increase in your clarity of understanding.

www.jamiesmart.com/results12

13

The Only Two Challenges that Stop People Making Progress

Overthinking: the art of creating problems that aren't even there.

Internet meme

'Where do you believe your experience is coming from?'

I was due to collect my car and take my daughters for dinner and a movie, but when I got to the garage, the car wasn't ready.

My head was swirling with urgency and reproach. *Why didn't I arrange to pick the car up earlier? Why did I try to squeeze so much in today? Why do I always do this?* I started pacing around the garage when suddenly, a quiet voice spoke from the depths of my being. . .

'*Where do you believe your experience is coming from?*'

I stopped in my tracks. '*Did you believe your feelings were letting you know about the car, or the movie, or your daughters? Did you believe your feelings were letting you know about your past, or your future, or what you're like as a person?*'

In a heartbeat, I fell out of contaminated thinking and into the moment. I called my ex-wife, explained I'd be late and asked her to feed the girls. I told her I'd be picking them up shortly and taking them to the movie.

The solution to my predicament was obvious once I fell out of contaminated thinking. We're built for reality. Our intelligence and wisdom is always there, ready to guide us the moment we wake up to reality. The only thing that gets in the way is contaminated thinking, arising from the outside-in misunderstanding. You're about to realize the only two challenges that ever stop people making progress.

Challenge one: Preoccupation

When I first meet a prospective client, they're typically preoccupied with something. This preoccupation can take many forms, but one thing's usually clear; they've been thinking about it. A lot! Brooding, ruminating, trying to figure it out. Here are some examples of the kinds of things people have been thinking far too much about:

- I want to get slim, fit and healthy, but I keep falling back into bad habits.

- I'm trying to find the right relationship (or fix my current one).

- I want to transition from my job to something more fulfilling and 'on-purpose'.

- I need to get more clients, but I don't know how.

- I want to play a bigger game but I don't know what it is.

- I'm trying to find my purpose in life, my true calling.

- I want to spend less time at the office and more time with my family.

- I need to change our company culture but nothing seems to work.

By the time they get to me, they've usually chewed it over, written checklists and ordered multiple books from Amazon about it. Sometimes they've made progress in all kinds of other areas, but *there's this one thing* that they just don't feel they're progressing with (or at least, not in the way they want to).

Challenge two: Underestimation

Similarly, when I first meet my clients, they tend to radically underestimate their talents, abilities and innate capacities, particularly in the area where they're preoccupied. Typically, they have a number of aspects of their life where they do really well. If we go through their personal histories, we find numerous examples of stellar qualities, including. . .

- Natural leadership

- Creativity and innovation

- Wisdom, intuition and gut feel

- Resilience and resourcefulness

- High performance

- Love, connection, kindness and compassion

- Realization and insight

It sometimes takes a little time and curiosity to find them, but they're *always* there. Yet when it comes to the area of their lives where they've been perceiving themselves as 'stuck' or 'struggling', people tend to overlook the fact that they're connected to these powerful resources.

The unexpected solution

So why do people get stuck in these two challenges in the first place? The answer to this is simple: contaminated thinking arising from the outside-in misunderstanding. This profoundly deceptive 'trick of the mind' is responsible for challenges one and two, and is the cause of the majority of problems we face as individuals, organizations and societies. The solution is a deeper embodied understanding of the principles behind clarity; an intuitive feel for the inside-out nature of how your mind and perception *already works*.

Implication-based learning

Implication-Based Learning (IBL) is the learning that takes place *automatically* when you're exposed to sensory data. Obvious examples include how you learned to walk and talk, even though no-one 'taught' you how to do them.

Gravity

Gravity is a pre-existing fact of life. From the moment you were born, the implications of gravity were 'obvious', so an *automatic* IBL curve was initiated. You now have a deep, *embodied understanding* of the implications of gravity; you use it automatically many times each day. That's how powerful your grounding in the *fact* of gravity is; a grounding that you developed effortlessly and automatically through IBL and benefit from *without even thinking about it.*

> *When you learn by implication,*
> *application is automatic. . .*

Germs

Germs are a pre-existing fact of life. We're born into a world of germs but, *unlike* gravity, germs are non-obvious. So before an automatic IBL curve can be initiated, germs and bacteria need to be made 'visible' to us (as children, this is accomplished by teaching us to 'hallucinate' germs). Somebody made germs visible to you, and an automatic IBL curve was initiated. Eventually, application became automatic. In fact, you've probably relied on your *embodied understanding* of germs and bacteria to do dozens of things in the past seven days, without even thinking about it (e.g. washing your hands, cleaning a surface). That's how powerful your grounding in the *fact* of germs is; a grounding that you developed using IBL and benefit from daily *without even thinking about it* consciously.

> *When you learn by implication,*
> *application is automatic. . .*

The principles behind clarity

Like gravity, the principles behind clarity are a pre-existing fact of life. You're born into them. But *unlike* gravity, the principles are non-obvious; they're invisible. The purpose of this book (and of all my work) is to make these principles 'visible' to you so that an automatic IBL curve is initiated, and you start benefiting from a deep embodied understanding of subtractive psychology. That way, *application becomes automatic*. As your embodied understanding of the principles behind clarity deepens, you get to benefit from that understanding throughout your day *without even thinking about it*. This is the source of the kind of clarity that leads to meaningful results.

Domain	Pre-existing fact of life?	Obvious?	IBL curve
Gravity	✓	✓	Initiated automatically via IBL
Germs and bacteria	✓	✗	Need to make it 'visible' first, then it progresses automatically via IBL
Inside-out nature of life/ the principles behind clarity	✓	✗	Need to make it 'visible' first, then it progresses automatically via IBL

There are aspects of life where you *already* perform brilliantly; where you trust yourself to respond intuitively in the moment. The difference between the areas where you struggle and the areas where you thrive is simple:

In the areas where you thrive, there's very little gap between your embodied understanding and reality.

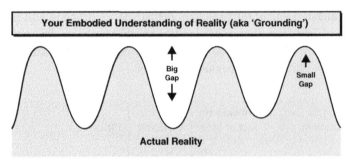

Figure 13.1:   Grounding: Your Embodied Understanding of Reality

Your mind is a self-correcting system

We all have places in our lives where we have a good embodied understanding of the self-correcting nature of our minds. Have you ever said something like one of the following?

- 'I'll sleep on it and see how the situation looks in the morning.'

- 'I'm not thinking clearly; I'll call them when I'm not feeling so annoyed.'

- 'I'm not getting anywhere. I'm going to take a break and come back to it with fresh eyes.'

These kinds of statements represent your *intuitive* understanding of the self-correcting nature of the mind. It's just that until now, you may not have realized just how reliably your state of mind can return to clarity. As you continue deepening your understanding of these principles, you're going to benefit from this innate capacity more and more.

So what's this got to do with impact?

Grounding is the foundational piece that allows you to have a profound, transformational impact on another person. When you listen to people who are extremely successful in a given field, you'll hear them pointing to an intuitive understanding of these principles (their grounding) without even realizing it. . .

'You miss 100% of the shots you don't take.' (Wayne Gretsky)

'There is only one way to avoid criticism: do nothing, say nothing, and be nothing.' (Aristotle)

'We don't see things as they are, we see them as we are.' (Anaïs Nin)

Like gravity, the principles behind clarity aren't something you 'do' or 'apply'; they're already there; something you realize for yourself. These principles are already playing out in your work, your relationships and in every other aspect of life.

> *You're already swimming in the intelligence and*
> *wisdom of life. We're living in these*
> *principles like fish are living in water.*

Your grounding is what governs the impact you're able to have, and how you're able to leverage it. I often speak to aspiring coaches and other transformation professionals who are passionate about making a difference to others. They know what they'd love to do, but say they don't know how to make a living from it. What initially looks like a commercial problem (e.g. 'How do I get clients?') usually turns out to be a grounding issue. As your grounding deepens, you find it much easier to resolve the commercial challenges.

Practicality check: How is understanding these two challenges going to help me get results?

In the domains where we're stuck in the outside-in misunderstanding, our minds are preoccupied with spurious causes, and we innocently underestimate our innate capacity for clarity, wisdom and insight. In the domains where our embodied understanding is more

---

closely aligned with the inside-out nature of life, we realize our innate capacities, thrive and create the results that matter to us. Misunderstanding complexifies; understanding simplifies.

CLARITY   equals   **CAPACITY**   minus   **CONTAMINATION**

Figure 13.2: The CLARITY® Equation

Your innate capacity for realization deepens your grounding by bringing you more closely into alignment with reality. The more aligned with reality you are, the easier it is to make progress and create results. So once you're making progress, what do you do on those occasions when you get knocked off-track?

Bottom line results: 'Institutionalized overthinking' is an occupational hazard for many organizations. Agile companies are less preoccupied and more aligned with their innate capacities. Everyone in your organization has the capacity to realize the one way the mind already works, and wake up to the truth of their innate capacity for clarity, insight and high performance.

keep exploring ⁘ *connect with others*
share your discoveries ⁘ *deepen your understanding*

Experiment: Identify some of the areas in your life where you already flourish and thrive. These are areas where you already have an intuitive understanding of the principles we're exploring. Isn't it nice to know that you already have places in your life where you deeply get this?

www.jamiesmart.com/results13

14

Finding Your Bearings When You Get Knocked Off-track

....

DANGER: Keep your fingers out of the machinery.

Health and safety notice

'You're going to have to raise your game. . .'

It was the end of the first hour of a one-to-one coaching intensive with Jim Lewcock, CEO of The Specialist Works. We were just about to go for a break when Jim dropped his bombshell, 'You're just regurgitating your book; you're going to have to raise your game'. I thanked him for being forthright with me, and said I'd reflect on what he'd said. *What was I going to do?* I thought I'd already been bringing my A-game for the past hour, but I didn't seem to be having much impact. I felt worried and anxious. *What if I wasn't up to it? What if I couldn't help my client?* The feelings of worry and anxiety were getting stronger when I suddenly realized what was going on. . .

> *Your feelings aren't telling you about your client, your past, your future or what you're like as a person. . .*
> *Your feelings are an experience of the principle of* THOUGHT *taking form right now, in this very moment.*

As the realization landed, my body started to relax and I began reflecting on the first hour of our session. Maybe he was feeling under pressure to get maximum value from this investment of his time, money and trust. Suddenly, inspiration struck; I knew what to do.

When Jim and I reconvened, I told him I'd realized what the problem was. I said, 'You're here for transformation. You want results, but you're not going to get them by collecting a bunch of new concepts and ideas. The thing that's going to make a difference to you is a *realization*; a deeper insight into the nature of your mind and your life. It's not going to come from me, my stories or my concepts; it's going to come from *inside you*. If you want that, you're going to need to raise *your* game and find a new way of listening'.

As I spoke the truth I was seeing in the moment, Jim fell out of his urgent, outside-in thinking and back into reality. The feeling of connection we'd had during our intake call re-emerged, and we started to make progress.

Your mind is a self-correcting system

We all lose our bearings from time to time, whether it's dealing with a difficult relationship, handling an unexpected situation or supporting a challenging client. But fortunately, your mind is a self-correcting system. We each have a kind of 'inner sat-nav' that allows us to keep our bearings when the going gets rough, and return to clarity quickly when we *do* temporarily lose our way.

Imagine a river that's being polluted by sewage from the outflow pipe of a factory. Upstream from the factory, the river still flows clear and pure. But downstream, the river is contaminated with toxic waste and the wildlife is suffering. Downstream, you could do your very best to clean the riverbanks and heal the wildlife, but your efforts would have no lasting effect while the factory is still contaminating the water with its noxious sewage. The solution is clear: *shut down the factory!* As its toxic output starts reducing, the river becomes less and less contaminated, and something wonderful starts to happen; the natural ecosystem starts to *cleanse and heal itself.*

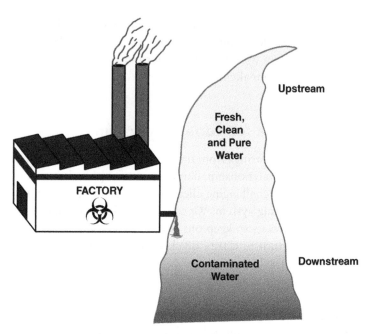

Figure 14.1: The River of Perception

And how is it able to cleanse and heal itself? Because at the river's *source* is a flow of fresh, clean, pure water. Whenever the outflow of contamination is stopped, even for a moment, the source of fresh clean water starts refreshing the ecosystem and clarity emerges. Why? Because clarity is the water's natural state.

Clarity is your mind's natural state.

I don't usually 'unpack' analogies, but this one is worth looking at directly. . .

- The outside-in misunderstanding is the 'factory' that contaminates the river.

- Contaminated thinking is the 'sewage' the factory produces.

- The river's source is MIND, the intelligent energy behind life.

- The river is the principle of THOUGHT, creating our perceptual experience and connecting us to that source.

- Attempts to clean the river are the *additive*, outside-in methods we use to try to change our felt experience, *after* it's been contaminated (the psychological equivalent of trying to un-bake a cake).

- Shutting down the factory represents the *subtractive* effect of a deeper embodied understanding of the principles behind clarity.

Sydney Banks points repeatedly to the principle of THOUGHT as the creative agent that unites us with the world we perceive, and with the source of all experience, saying: 'THOUGHT is the missing link that gives us the power to recognize the illusionary separation between the spiritual world and the world of form.'

Your experience flows from and is directly connected to MIND, the source of fresh, pure perception.

When you fall out of contaminated thinking, even for a moment. . .
That source of pure being starts refreshing your aware-
ness, and clarity emerges.
THOUGHT is the river that unites you with the world you
perceive, and with the source of pure being.

How to clear your mind

Your mind is a self-correcting system. The only thing that *ever* slows the process of self-correction is the mistaken belief that we're feeling something *other than* THOUGHT in the moment. So what do you need to do to clear your mind? Keep your fingers out of the machinery and continue deepening your understanding of subtractive psychology. As your insights and realizations continue to update your embodied understanding, you'll find your mind's self-correcting system restoring you to clarity more and more quickly and easily.

A dangerous assignment

We're always living in the feeling of THOUGHT in the moment, even when it *appears as if* our feelings are coming from somewhere else. As soon as we assign our feelings to a cause *other than* THOUGHT in the moment, we innocently reinforce the *false belief* that we are separate from and at the mercy of a world 'out there' in space and time, with power over how we feel. It then seems sensible that we look 'out there' for a solution.

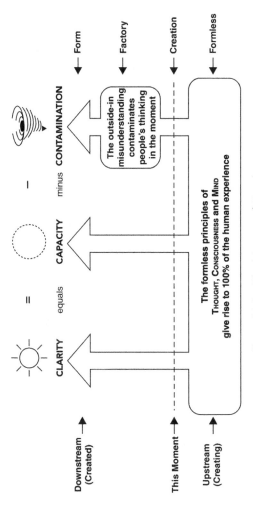

Figure 14.2: The Moment of Creation

We *all* get tricked by the outside-in misunderstanding; we're innocently walking around in a THOUGHT-generated percep-tual reality, and relating to it as an *actual* reality. But as you continue waking up from this misunderstanding, you're going to find yourself falling out of contaminated thinking more and more quickly and easily. And when you fall out of a contami-nated Narnia, where you land is *reality*.

Just as we were born into the principle of gravity, we were
born into the principle of THOUGHT.
And just as all seven billion people on the planet are
wandering around in gravity. . .
All seven billion of us are wandering around in THOUGHT.

So what does this have to do with impact?

Clarity of connection and clarity of thought are universal. We all have times when we experience a deep connection to others, and an effortlessly clear mind. But as you continue deepen-ing your clarity of understanding, you're going to find your-self *effortlessly* spending more time in the moment, with your innate self-correcting system waking you up when you *do* get caught up in your thinking.

Your impact is a function of your clarity of thought,
connection and understanding.
As your level of consciousness continues increasing. . .

Realization and insight will return you to the present moment. . .
The domain of clarity, connection and impact.

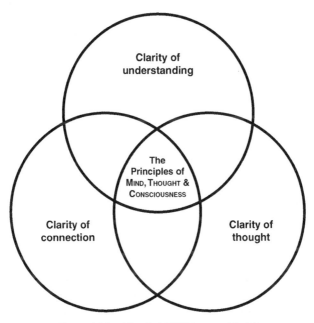

Figure 14.3: The CLARITY® Impact Model

Think less, achieve more

A lot has happened in the three years since Jim's coaching intensive. For instance, Jim decided to purchase one of his competitors (a multi-million-pound risk). Their clarity of understanding meant he and his team were able to move quickly, win over the new employees and double the company's profits in one year. When The Specialist Works' 100 staff were moving to new premises, Jim had a sudden realization that led to him inviting his *employees* to design their new workspaces. The result is an office space that's inherently connected to the company culture, deep engagement from the staff who spend so much of their lives there and a six-figure saving on design fees.

The advertising industry always has unsold capacity, so Jim had an insight and created Goodwill Rocks. He persuaded 20 media companies each to donate £50,000 worth of media assets, then invited large charities to join them. Twenty large charities got involved right away, so The Specialist Works is now doing business with the charitable sector. Goodwill Rocks is accomplishing in *months* what would have taken Jim's team *years* to do using traditional thinking, and has already created a million pounds' worth of value for charities. The Specialist Works ended up being selected as one of the *Sunday Times 100 Best Small Companies to Work For*. When I asked him about this, Jim said the reason was simple. 'When You're authentically engaged, stuff really works.'

Practicality check: How is my mind's self-correcting system going to help me get results?

As you continue to have realizations and insights into your innate capacities, your ability to create results increases radically. . .

- The subtractive nature of this understanding means you have less on your mind.

- With less on your mind, you're more available to realization, wisdom and insight, the source of the best ideas.

- You start to feel more connected with others, better able to listen, serve and impact them.

- You also start getting clearer on what really matters to you, unlocking your inner source of authentic power.

- You may even find yourself tapping into a deeper well of inspiration, motivation and courage, a powerful mix when it comes to taking action to create the results that matter to you. Remember. . .

| CLARITY | plus | ACTION | equals | RESULTS |

Figure 14.4:   The CLARITY® Results Model

So how do you tune in to the kind of wisdom and common sense that leads to transformational results?

Bottom line results: The mind is a self-correcting system, evolved to *automatically* default to clarity. While it's inevitable that you'll get caught up in contaminated thinking from time to time, it's also inevitable that your mind will self-correct to clarity.

keep exploring ⁖ connect with others
share your discoveries ⁖ deepen your understanding

Experiment: In the 'river' metaphor, we explored the notion that the principle of THOUGHT is an unbroken connection between the world of form that we perceive, and the fresh, pure source that gives rise to our perception. What happens when you reflect on the fact that this is happening *right now*, in your experience, second by second?

www.jamiesmart.com/results14

15

Making Good Decisions: Wisdom, Intuition and Common Sense

....

Follow the wisdom that's inside, because you know as much about truth as any other human being.

Sydney Banks, Author, philosopher, welder

'I don't know. . .'

My client had come to me because he was stuck, and didn't know how to move forward with his life. He'd been trying to make an important decision for many months, but the more he'd thought about it, the more entrenched he'd become. But now that same sense of stuck-ness had permeated our coaching session. My questions were easy, but my client's answers kept coming back the same way. 'I don't know.' My clear head and good feeling were rapidly being replaced with stress and irritation. *Why couldn't he just have a guess? He was a bright guy; why was he being so difficult? Why wouldn't he just answer my questions?* We were *both* stuck. He didn't know what to answer, and I didn't know how else to engage him. As my frustration grew, a new thought popped into my mind. . .

Where do you believe your experience is coming from?

In a flash, I fell out of the La-la Land of my judgemental, contaminated thinking and landed back in reality. 'Your feelings aren't letting you know about a difficult *client*', I realized, 'they're letting you know about difficult *thinking*; the principle of THOUGHT taking a "frustrated" form in the moment.'

When you fall out of the illusory non-reality of contaminated thinking. . .
Where you come to rest is the present moment; the reality you're built for. . .
A domain rich with wisdom, intuition and common sense.

When it comes to deciding what's right for you and your life, nobody has more access to wisdom than you. As you start tuning in to this 'common sense', you'll realize just how ever-present and available it is when you're free from mental clutter.

How to make good decisions

As the world becomes more complex, volatile and uncertain, the consequences of our decisions become increasingly ambiguous, and we all have times when we find them challenging to make. But here's the thing: while different decisions bring different consequences and levels of complexity, there's nothing in *reality* that makes one decision more difficult than another. . .

The outside-in misunderstanding is the main source of difficulty in decision making. . .
But as you fall out of the complexity of contaminated thinking. . .
You fall into the simplicity of wisdom and common sense.

People aren't good at predicting emotional responses

Research reveals that people do poorly when it comes to predicting their emotional states in future scenarios. We fall prey to a variety of cognitive biases, amplifying our expected emotional response to *certain* things while underplaying or even *ignoring* others. While we can passionately believe that we would feel terrible if X happened or wonderful if Y happened, the truth is more fundamental: remember, you can't be a victim of circumstance, and neither can anyone else. We're always going to be living in the experience of THOUGHT in the moment, no matter what.

DISTINCTION: Good luck vs bad luck

There's an old Taoist story about a farmer whose prize mare runs away. 'What bad luck,' the farmer's neighbours commiserate, but he replies, 'Maybe, maybe not.' The next day, the horse returns with a powerful stallion following behind. 'What a fortunate man you are,' the neighbours say as the farmer and his son corral the two horses, but he is again philosophical: 'Maybe, maybe not.' Later that day, the farmer's son falls and breaks his leg while attempting to tame the wild stallion. 'That really *is* rotten luck,' the neighbours tut, but (to their annoyance) the farmer replies, 'Maybe, maybe not.' A few days later, a general and his troops come to the village and conscript all the young men to fight at the front. All except the farmer's son, who stays at home because of his broken leg. 'You have to admit, that was incredibly lucky,' the bewildered neighbours say, shaking their heads at the farmer's mysterious powers as he replies predictably. . .

'Maybe, maybe not. . .'

While 100% of your feelings are generated from within, the optical illusion of the mind can make it *seem* like they come from the outside; from somewhere *other than* THOUGHT in the moment. While the neighbours perceived the farmer's life as a wild pendulum of good fortune and bad, the farmer remained composed and philosophical. It can absolutely seem like your security and wellbeing is coming from circumstances (e.g. money, jobs, romantic partners), the future (e.g. hopes, fears, uncertainties), the past (e.g. victories, defeats, indiscretions) and even yourself (e.g. physique, health, personality). But all of those factors are *neutral*. 100% of your feelings are generated from within; you're living in the experience of the principle of THOUGHT taking form in the moment.

Reality check

So am I saying it doesn't matter what you decide? No, I'm not. The choices you make can have an enormous effect on your life and the lives of others, today and 20 years from today. Your ability to make good decisions is infinitely improved when you're *not* being hamstrung by contamination from the outside-in misunderstanding. When you're hanging out in reality, you *intuitively* realize what you've got going for you.

Freedom from fear of public speaking

I was working with a client who was scheduled to give a talk to a large audience, and was suffering with anticipatory anxiety. The person genuinely believed their feelings were giving them feedback about the future event. This despite the fact that the future event didn't exist in *reality*; it only existed as a plan in the present. While there was certainly a high degree of probability that the event would happen, the talk would not exist in any real or factual way until several weeks later, when the client walked onto the stage. There was no place in the client's present *reality* where the talk existed; it only existed as an idea. While they could certainly *believe* they were feeling the future event, they were actually feeling THOUGHT in the moment.

The issue isn't that we sometimes have uncomfortable feelings arising from THOUGHT *in the moment. . .*
The issue is that we sometimes believe there's more to it than that. . .
That our feelings are arising from something other than THOUGHT *in the moment.*

Think about it: if you tell someone you're in a particular state of mind (e.g. happy, sad, excited, angry, grateful, stressed, love), they typically ask a variant of 'Why?' or 'What about?' We've been innocently conditioned to look to the outside for a reason. Whether the 'outside' we point to is our circumstances, the past or the future. Whether it's our physical body, our personality or our habits. We've been trained to look away from the true source of power that's *creating* our experience, and assign the cause somewhere else. We feel a feeling and assume, 'There's no smoke without fire; there must be *something* out there that's causing this.' But the world of form is neutral; it's totally incapable of creating a feeling. Your experience is the creation of THOUGHT in the moment, brought to life by CONSCIOUSNESS. When it comes to our feelings, there *is* smoke without fire. The smoke of our feelings is giving us moment-to-moment feedback about the ebb and flow of THOUGHT, *not* about the 'fire' of circumstances, past, present or future. And it raises an important question. . .

What quality of decision making can you expect when a person is basing their decisions on misinformation?

When people mistakenly believe in a La-la Land, many of their predictions and decisions are fundamentally flawed, contaminated by misinformation. For example. . .

- When people mistakenly believed in a *flat earth (La-la Land)*. . .

- When astronomers mistakenly believed in a *geocentric universe (La-la Land)*. . .

- When chemists mistakenly believed combustion was caused by *phlogiston (La-la Land)*. . .

- When doctors *mistakenly believed* infection was caused by *miasmas (La-la Land)*, with disastrous consequences for their patients' physical health. . .

Similarly, when you and I *mistakenly believe* in an *outside-in world* (La-la Land), many of our predictions and decisions are fundamentally flawed, contaminated by misinformation.

Reality check

'Wait a minute. . .' I hear you say. 'What about when someone gives me the creeps, or I suddenly get the sense that I shouldn't go down a particular street. Are you really saying that's just THOUGHT?' Yes and no. We have our senses for a reason; they give us essential information about reality that we calibrate to so we can survive and thrive. When you're present and aware, THOUGHT is free to do what it does best: guide you through reality in this game we call life.

Practicality check: How are wisdom, intuition and common sense going to help me get results?

It stands to reason that the decisions we perceive as most important are often the ones where we get tricked by the outside-in illusion. Misunderstanding adds an *exponential* level of complexity to any decision. Conversely, *understanding simplifies*, subtracting contaminated thinking, and waking you up to the wisdom and common sense you were born with.

CLARITY plus **ACTION** equals **RESULTS**

Figure 15.1: The CLARITY® Results Model

The moment I woke up to reality, everything changed. Feelings of humility and compassion washed over me as my client transformed before my eyes from 'difficult and uncooperative' to 'feeling insecure and doing the best he can'. I was guided in how to work with him, and as he fell out of contaminated thinking, he suddenly got clarity on the way forward for him. Once you're navigating by wisdom, you're all set to take your results to a whole new level.

Bottom line results: It can be both humbling and enlightening to realize that a percentage of the decisions we've made in our lives have been based on *misinformation*; 'noise in the system' arising from the outside-in misunderstanding. While misunderstanding adds complexity to decision making, understanding simplifies. It subtracts complexity and reconnects you with reality, wisdom and common sense.

keep exploring ❖ connect with others
share your discoveries ❖ deepen your understanding

Experiment: What are some of the times when you suddenly realized the answer to something that you had struggled with until that point? It can be empowering to discover that your capacity for insight and realization is innate. As your understanding continues to deepen, you're going to find yourself coming to rely on it more and more.

www.jamiesmart.com/results15

16

The Source of Impact, Innovation and Disruption

Today, if you're not disrupting yourself, someone else is; your fate is to be either the disrupter or the disrupted. There is no middle ground.

Salim Ismail, Author, entrepreneur and angel investor

'"Uber protest" by black cab drivers brings traffic chaos to Westminster. . .'

The *Guardian* headline from 26 May 2015 reported black cab drivers' protest against Uber, the app that's rapidly disrupting the taxi trade in over 700 cities around the world. But from the moment the first consumer satellite navigation systems started coming on the market in the 1990s, the writing was on the wall for London's iconic black cab.

Airbnb.com was valued at $30 billion in August 2016, making it more valuable than Hyatt Hotels or the InterContinental Hotels Group (owner of Holiday Inn and Crowne Plaza). But the potential for an Airbnb was in the wind from the early 2000s, as Web 2.0 started giving rise to the virtual communities, social networking sites and user-generated content of the 'sharing economy'.

The music industry's revenues dropped by 50% between 2001 and 2010. The executives held tight to their outdated business model, like sailors in a hurricane clinging to the mast of their sinking ship. But as far back as 1999, Napster and other file-sharing services were foreshadowing the storm that would decimate the music business.

One of the reasons there are so few Ubers, iTunes and Airbnbs is because of how very *difficult* it is to accurately predict the future. So what's the source of impact, innovation and disruption? Exponential insight. As you get a deeper understanding of exponential insight, you unlock its power to create competitive advantage and exponential results.

The strategy equation

I was scheduled to deliver the keynote speech to kick off a strategy workshop for the council of the Institute and Faculty of Actuaries (IFoA). The IFoA has over 25,000 members, and its council had been charged with developing strategy for the future of the profession. Actuaries are renowned for being extremely detail-oriented, data-driven and analytical; they also love playing devil's advocate. The chief executive wanted me to inspire some fresh thinking, new perspectives and innovative ideas. I reflected to myself. . .

- How can you meet these people where they are?

- How can you make it easy for them to look in the direction you're pointing?

- How can you make it a no-brainer for them to come on the journey?

Early in the talk, I told them about Airbnb, Hyatt and the exponential impact of digital technology. I told them about Allstate Insurance, which had put up a $10,000 prize for the first team who could beat its insurance algorithm (an algorithm developed over 60 years by some of the world's finest actuaries and data scientists). More than 100 teams competed for the prize, and after *three months* Allstate's algorithm had been optimized by over 270%, saving the company tens of millions of dollars in annual costs. Allstate had the data, but that was only half the formula.

Now I had their attention. I asked them if they'd like to know the formula for strategy, and they nodded eagerly. I wrote. . .

$$STRATEGY = DATA + INSIGHT$$

They assured me that they were already great at gathering and analysing data, but that they weren't so familiar with insight. So I asked them, 'When do you get your best ideas?' I've asked thousands of people this question, and the answers are always the same. . .

– In the shower	– Walking or running	– Connecting with other people
– Dropping off to sleep	– Sitting by the ocean	– When I stop thinking about a problem
– Travelling to and from work	– On holiday	– When I'm doing something else
		– etc

We're *built* for exponential insight! You've been having insights and realizations your whole life, but when we attribute them to external factors (walks, woods, workouts) we limit our understanding of just how available insight is. As you reflect on some of the realizations that have already made a big difference to you in your life, you'll start to realize just what a powerful source of intelligence you have going for you. And that's good because. . .

We are now living in a VUCA world

The acronym VUCA was coined by the US Army War College to describe the kinds of scenarios the military have been finding themselves in since the 1990s. The term has been adopted more recently by businesses and futurists because we *all* now live in a VUCA world: a domain of *volatility, uncertainty, complexity* and *ambiguity.*

Alfred Korzybski (creator of general semantics) served as an intelligence officer during the First World War. He realized that while the *technology* of war was progressing at an astonishing rate, the social structures, organizations and habits of thinking that gave *rise* to the war were not progressing. In the 100 years since Korzybski's insight, our technology has kept accelerating exponentially, but our societal understanding of thinking and perception is still stuck in the Middle Ages.

At our current level of consciousness, entrusting humanity with exponential technology is like giving a toddler a loaded machine gun.
We need a new understanding of how our minds work to navigate the challenges of volatility, uncertainty, complexity and ambiguity.

DISTINCTION: Linear thinking vs exponential insight

Computing power grows **exponentially**: it doubles in speed and halves in size and cost roughly every two years (a function known as Moore's Law). Our *intellects* have evolved for the **linear** world we've lived in for most of human history. But digital technology is driving us at high speed into a VUCA world that requires a new, more leveraged way of thinking.

While **linear thinking** can be useful, it has an inherent limitation: its only reference point is the past; the thoughts you've *already* had. All too often, we approach strategy, goal setting and problem solving by identifying problems and solutions from our *current* level of consciousness, then setting out to solve them from the same perspective. By definition, **linear thinking** is blind to the present moment, and the implications of what's happening *right now*. We're riding the wave of the information revolution; a wave powered by **exponential** technology. When Airbnb launched in August 2008, the team didn't have access to better *data* than Hyatt. They didn't have a bigger budget or more experience. What they *did* have was **exponential insight**: realizations that aligned them with reality and allowed them to invent the future.

Stephen Hawking, Elon Musk and Bill Gates have all expressed concern about the enormous risks to humanity that artificial intelligence poses. We have to recognize and harness the power of **exponential insight** if we want to sense and respond to the challenges of the digital age. We have to understand the *nature* of THOUGHT if we are to survive and thrive as individuals, as organizations, as societies and as a *species*.

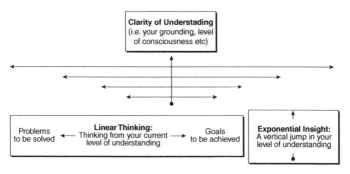

Figure 16.1:   Exponential Insights Enable Exponential Results

William Duggan (a senior lecturer in business at Columbia Business School) attributes the dubious popularity of the 'audacious goals, unwavering self-belief and massive action' school of thought (see Chapter 7) to a rags-to-riches myth that's been recycled by 'success gurus' since the 1800s. He suggests that a much more rational approach is to prepare for opportunity, see it when it shows up and act on it. Duggan explains that when you prepare for opportunity, you open yourself to the arrival of flashes of realization; the exponential insights that are found over and over again at the source of some of the biggest achievements in history, from Archimedes' bathtub 'Eureka!' to Bill Gates' insight into the future of computing.

As you continue exploring the inside-out nature of reality, you'll find yourself opening to the same source of exponential insight used by great results-creators throughout history.

Practicality check: How is exponential insight going to help me get results?

Most success in human endeavours comes from insight, experimentation and acting on opportunity when it arises. In order to act on an opportunity, you need to be aware of and prepared for it. As your understanding of subtractive psychology continues to evolve, you're going to have more awareness of the present moment, the domain of reality, clarity and exponential insight.

So as your interpersonal transformation continues, it's time to ignite your *commercial* transformation.

Bottom line results: We're used to linear thinking, but we need exponential insight to deal with the challenges of a world of volatility, uncertainty, complexity and ambiguity (VUCA). Exponential insights are a source of massive leverage because they bring you and your organization more closely into alignment with reality.

---

keep exploring ⁘ *connect with others share your discoveries* ⁘ *deepen your understanding*

Experiment: When do you get your best ideas? What happens when you open to the possibility that you're always connected to the source of exponential insight?

www.jamiesmart.com/results16

PART THREE

LEVERAGE
Your Commercial Transformation

You never change things by fighting the existing reality. To change something, build a new model that makes the existing model obsolete.

R. Buckminster Fuller
Designer and inventor

Hope lies in dreams, in imagination, and in the courage of those who dare to make dreams into reality.

Jonas Salk
Virologist, inventor of the polio vaccine

LEVERAGE
Your Commercial Transformation

17

Ignite Your Entrepreneurial Instincts

Most people are walking around, umbilical cord in hand, looking for a new place to plug it in.

Cavett Robert, Founder of the National Speakers Association

'You are the leader of your life, and you always have been. . .'

The insight hit me like a ton of bricks. I'd been working as a programme manager, leading multi-million-pound business transformation projects for five years. It was a good job but

I felt stuck. Some of my friends had left their jobs to go self-employed or start their own businesses, but I was convinced that 'doing my own thing' wasn't possible for me. I didn't question why; it just seemed true.

Everything changed one weekend in 1998 when I attended a workshop to improve my influence skills. The trainer stood at the front of the room, relaxed and at ease, sharing engaging stories and insightful perspectives. Watching this skilled 'transformation professional', my first thought was, 'I want to be able to do that'. I became completely absorbed in the learning experience, and at some point in the weekend, I had a profound and liberating insight:

You are the leader of your life, and you always have been.
You can choose the results you want to create,
and live into the choices you make.

I found a contracting role that would give me the extra time and money I needed to pursue my new-found dream of becoming a facilitator, speaker and coach, then I handed in my notice. I took every opportunity I could find to step out of my comfort zone, create value for the organization and grow. I coached my colleagues, ran in-house project management workshops and offered to facilitate challenging meetings for the company directors. It turns out that paid employment can be a great 'sandbox' where you get rewarded for creating value while you learn and practice *today* the skills you're going to need *tomorrow*.

After two years of awakening my entrepreneurial instincts, I stopped contracting and started my first business. So what *are* your entrepreneurial instincts? They're expressions of the deep drivers we started exploring in Chapters 1 and 6 (direction, resilience, creativity, authenticity, intuition, presence, connection and clarity).

Implications drive instincts

As you have realizations into the 100% inside-out nature of how the mind *already works*, you reignite the entrepreneurial instincts that have been with you your whole life. . .

IMPLICATION 1: You can't be a victim of circumstance

As you realize it's impossible for you to be a victim of circumstance, you become less likely to look to the outside world for security, approval and validation. Fear of failure and fear of criticism are revealed to be all bark and no bite. It becomes easier to take calculated risks, free from confusion about where your wellbeing comes from. You become more carefree, enjoying yourself and having fun as you experiment and explore. As you take action, you take responsibility for creating the results you want to create.

IMPLICATION 2: You're wired for realization; you're an insight machine

As you come to rely on your innate capacity for realization, you start trusting that you're going to have the insights you need when you need them. This innate capacity for realization is the source of innovative solutions to problems. It allows you to see 'the elusive obvious', both at the micro-scale, and at the macro-scale of massive vision and purpose. Reality is changing fast, so it can be a huge relief to discover that you're built to have fresh new perceptions that bring you more closely into alignment with that reality as it evolves.

IMPLICATION 3: We each live in a separate reality

As you start to see that we each live in our own, THOUGHT-generated perceptual reality, the whole domain of 'other people' becomes simplified. You'll start finding it easier to see things from others' perspective – to connect with them and 'get' their world – while staying true to yourself. Being able to understand what other people are up against is an entrepreneurial 'superpower' that allows you to identify opportunities, influence others, create solutions and get clients.

IMPLICATION 4: You're always connected to everyone and everything

As you realize you're always connected to your true self, to other people and to the whole of life, you discover you're an inherent part of this creative, evolutionary intelligence. The only thing that ever obscures this fact is contaminated thinking arising from the outside-in misunderstanding. Your dreams, desires and aspirations exist for a reason; you're part of life and you always have been. As you relax into the truth of this, you become more available to wisdom, realization and common sense. Feeling connected to who you really are, to other people and to life itself starts becoming the norm.

IMPLICATION 5: Your mind is a self-correcting system

As you continue realizing your mind's self-correcting nature, you'll find yourself falling out of contaminated thinking and waking up to reality, more and more quickly and easily. As you come to rely on this powerful capacity, you'll spend less time in unnecessary hesitation, worry and conflict. The result of this unburdening is greater agility and awareness. Decision-making becomes easier as you are freed from the misinformation of the outside-in misunderstanding.

IMPLICATION 6: You're built for reality and optimized for results

You're a born learner, with an extraordinary ability to sense, choose and take action. In fact, the vast majority of actions you take each day (e.g. walking, reading, talking) you do without even thinking about it, because of the depth of your embodied understanding. As your understanding of the principles behind clarity increases, you become more present and aware, with less on your mind. As a result you're going to find yourself sensing, choosing and acting more fully in alignment with what truly matters to you. This is the path to the kind of experiences and results truly worth having.

IMPLICATION 7: Your conception of the future is not reality; *now* is reality

While it can be wonderful to envision the future, it doesn't actually exist. Our ideas of the future are not reality; they never include the totality of our innate capacities, and of who we really are. As a result, we often overlook a simple fact:

You're built for the reality of the present moment. . .
When the future arrives, <u>it</u> will be the present moment. . .
The reality you're built for. . . the here and now.

People often ask me 'Why aren't we born knowing this?' But we are. The average four-year-old is far more 'psychologically healthy' than their parents or teenage siblings, intuitively embodying many of the qualities listed above. The *issue* is that we're conditioned into believing in a non-reality; the illusory La-la Land of the outside-in misunderstanding. This is why little children are more 'entrepreneurial' than most adults, and it's great news. Why?

As you deepen your understanding of the principles behind clarity, you reignite your entrepreneurial instincts.

So does this mean everyone can be a high-profile entrepreneur?

At the level of principle, yes, but in practice, there's a more important question. . . What would you love to have happen? What are you inspired to create? Often, I hear people repeating mantras like this. . .

- 'I'd do the things that really matter to me, but I haven't got the time.'

- 'I hate my job but I can't get work doing anything else.'

- 'I'd follow my heart if I was guaranteed it would work out OK.'

- 'I'd do what I love but I can't get paid for it.'

- 'I'd be happy if I could find work that fulfils me.'

- 'I'd do something meaningful if I knew how to do it.'

- 'I'd do what I love if only I knew what it was.'

The outside-in misunderstanding wafts through these statements like a bad smell, but as people start waking up from contaminated thinking, amazing things start to happen. You may. . .

- Discover that you *enjoy* the job you were previously desperate to leave.

- Find yourself working towards an inspiring result, just for the hell of it.

- Take on responsibilities that you'd previously tried to avoid.

- Change direction to do something that wasn't previously on your radar.

- Take action and do things that you wouldn't even have *considered* previously.

Entrepreneurs take responsibility

We opened this chapter with a pithy quote about umbilical cords. Twenty years ago, I would probably have told you the key was to plug that umbilical cord into *yourself*; to take 100% responsibility for yourself and your results. This is what many entrepreneurs do, and it's one of the reasons so many of them get stressed-out, burned out and find themselves back where they started within a couple of years.

While it's important to take responsibility, I now see it differently. Your 'umbilical cord' is *already* plugged into life itself. You're always connected to life and you always have been. If you're willing to take responsibility for (a) prioritizing your own evolution, (b) clearing up the misunderstandings that have been holding you back until now, and (c) moving forward boldly. . . then life will support you. Just as it has done every step of the way.

Practicality check: How is reigniting my entrepreneurial instincts going to help me get results?

Whether you're working in an existing structure or creating something brand new, your entrepreneurial instincts are what support you in doing something you've never done before. When you take action, your entrepreneurial instincts cut through the theory, and allow you to get impartial feedback from the real world.

So once you've reignited your entrepreneurial instincts, who are you going to make a difference to?

Bottom line results: Big companies are often told they should 'act like startups', but this is impractical advice. It makes far more sense for companies to cultivate *the freedom of thought* that startups benefit from by awakening the *entrepreneurial instincts* that are latent in the company's people. The commitment to purpose, willingness to experiment and focus on the customer experience that typify the 'startup mindset' emerge naturally when you ignite your entrepreneurial instincts.

keep exploring ⁙ connect with others
share your discoveries ⁙ deepen your understanding

Experiment: I invite you to open to the possibility that you already have entrepreneurial instincts. It may be some time since you've relied on them, but they're still there, waiting to be reignited. And how do you reignite them? Do something. Get started. When you take action from clarity, the way forward becomes clearer.

www.jamiesmart.com/results17

18

Tribal Marketing: Engaging Your Audience

....

The goal is not to do business with everybody who needs what you have.
The goal is to do business with people who believe what you believe.

Simon Sinek, Author, speaker

'Katherine's got clarity. . .'

I was feeling insecure about my lack of a 'social media strategy' before my first book *CLARITY* launched in 2013. The UK's biggest book retailer (WHSmith) had selected *CLARITY* as its

'Deal of the Week', so the book would be getting pride of place in railway stations, airports and motorway services across the UK. But while I had tens of thousands of people in my network, I didn't really 'get' social media. I was having coffee with my colleague Katherine on the day Amazon started delivering *CLARITY* into people's letterboxes when I had a flash of inspiration. I took a picture of her holding the book, then posted it to Facebook with the simple message 'Katherine's got clarity ;-)'

Within a few days, dozens of people had posted photos of themselves with the book and the 'got clarity' message. As the weeks passed, the photos became funnier and more creative, with people competing to post the best 'clarity photos'. This unanticipated viral outbreak continued to grow and, by the date of the WHSmith launch, there were countless clarity photos circulating on Facebook.

And that's when something interesting happened. A friend arrived at London's Heathrow Airport after several weeks' holiday to see enormous 'Deal of the Week' posters announcing the book. When he logged on to Facebook, his timeline was filled with pictures of people he knew, proudly displaying copies of *CLARITY*. He was shocked, and sent me a bewildered congratulatory message, saying, 'This is amazing. Your book is everywhere! How did you do it?'

But the book *wasn't* everywhere; it was everywhere in *his neighbourhood*. The members of his tribe had *CLARITY*, so when he stood among them, it seemed as though *everyone* had it.

The search for meaning, purpose and belonging

In the past, people looked to certain institutions to 'give them' a sense of security, purpose and belonging (e.g. church, government, school, monolithic companies, marriage, job for life etc). But as technological and sociological changes continue to sweep the globe, many of those institutions are failing to engage the communities they once served. As we are propelled into the VUCA world, people are searching for that sense of security, purpose and belonging, and they're finding it in tribes: communities of like-minded people who share their values and worldview. As a result, purpose, authenticity and transparency are becoming more important than ever because you can't *fake* authenticity. In a time of 24×7 social media and smartphones, people are going to see the real you, and this presents a huge opportunity.

When you're being who you really are, you shine a beacon
for those who align with you and your worldview.
Your purpose, authenticity and transparency send an
honest signal that resonates with others.

The spread of the internet and social media has meant that we *all* now have the power that used to be reserved for politicians, the news media and captains of industry. A teenager with a smartphone can now command an audience that only used to be available to the most popular TV shows. Management thinker Peter Drucker explained that a business has two core functions that create results: marketing and innovation. If marketing is a way of multiplying your ability to sell something, you can think of *tribal* marketing as a way of connecting with, engaging and giving value to a tribe who resonate with your worldview. When you have a highly engaged tribe, it becomes much more straightforward for them to 'buy' what you're offering. This is the case whether you're a student looking to promote club nights at your university or a CEO who wants to engage your colleagues and other stakeholders. . . whether you're a coach who's keen to build a community of potential colleagues and clients, or a marketing director seeking to create raving fans for your company's products and services.

Tribal leadership

Who are a group of people you want to serve? Becoming the leader of a tribe puts you in an extremely influential position. Members of the tribe will give you their attention, their loyalty, their time and their money on an ongoing basis *if* (and only if) you continue to show them that you are worthy of it, by. . .

- 'getting' their reality, understanding their worldview and genuinely caring about them

- helping them solve their problems, achieve their goals and get the results that matter to them

- being honest, authentic, transparent and trustworthy

- being courageous, true to yourself and doing what makes sense to you.

You show you're worthy of being the leader by <u>leading</u>. . .
By going first and giving value to the people you're
here to serve.

So what audience or group of people would you love to make a difference to? This isn't about 'finding your niche'; it's not even about *you*! It's about selecting a group of people you want to *serve*.

Every audience is another room in your mansion

Here's a way of thinking about it: imagine that you've inherited a large and beautiful mansion, with a trust fund paying the running costs. There's only one catch: if you want the trust fund to pay the bills, you have to restore the mansion's rooms, and they're in a shocking state, with torn wallpaper and broken chairs. They need cleaning, painting and plenty of tender loving care to return them to their former glory. So which room do you want to start with? The lounge or the master bedroom? The kitchen or the billiard room? Once that one's been taken care of, you can decide which one you want to do next. You don't have to *limit* yourself to one; you don't have to stay in it forever. You don't need to make the room part of your identity. You just need to decide which one you want to start with.

It's the same with audiences. You don't need to limit yourself to one, or stay with the same audience forever. You don't need to make the group part of your identity. But it can be very useful to choose which one you want to start with; a group you'd love to serve. Then, if you decide you want to increase your domain, you can decide which group you want to serve *next*. Every audience is another room in your mansion.

Remember, everyone is walking around in a separate reality; a THOUGHT-generated *perceptual* reality that they experience as an *actual* reality. People gravitate towards others who have perceptual realities similar to their own. A tribe is a group of people whose values and worldview are similar enough that they find it easy to connect with and relate to *each other*.

What's your story?

Tribal leaders tell *authentic* stories that resonate with the worldview and values of the people in their tribes. These stories turn *off* as many people as they turn *on*; they make it easy for someone to decide whether this tribe is for them or not. For example, in her TED talk, *The Art of Asking*, Amanda Palmer tells the story of her rise from street performer to rock star, and the importance of vulnerability, connection and the willingness to ask for help. Her story attracted plenty of criticism, but the people who resonated with her worldview knew instantly that she was someone they wanted to listen to. Many thousands of her tribe members engage with each other on dedicated Facebook groups *they've* created for the purpose.

Your authentic stories make it easier for people to connect with you and relate to you, establishing your credibility to lead the tribe. Why? Because the story you tell resonates with a story your tribe members are telling themselves (or *want* to tell themselves).

Practicality check: How is learning about tribal engagement going to help me get results?

The bigger the impact you want to have, the more likely you are to need the support of other people. Experience shows that people who resonate with your worldview, values and purpose are *far* more likely to support your efforts.

So once you know who you want to lead, how do you make a difference to them?

Bottom line results: Whether you're the CEO of a Fortune 500 company, or a transformation professional working with a select group of clients, there are certain audiences that it's critical for you to connect with. 'Getting' your audience's perceptual reality puts you in a powerful position to connect with and lead them. The more you're able to create value for your audience in a way that's honest, authentic and transparent, the happier they'll be to give you their attention, their trust, their loyalty, their money and their time.

keep exploring ⁙ connect with others
share your discoveries ⁙ deepen your understanding

Experiment: What's a group of people you/your organization would love to serve? Hint: they may be a group of people you're already well acquainted with; people whose values and worldview you share and understand.

www.jamiesmart.com/results18

19

The Only Things Anyone Ever Pays For

One man's meat is another man's poison.

Ancient proverb

'A True Fan is defined as someone who will purchase anything and everything you produce. . .'

In his legendary 2008 blog post '1000 True Fans', author Kevin Kelly suggested creators could make a decent living with just 1000 True Fans (people who will purchase anything and everything you produce), and explained that if these fans each spent $100 per year, it would generate a $100,000 income. And while his message spoke to the challenges faced by artists, there are valuable lessons in it for us all. When Kelly posted this, I'd already spent five years building a tribe of 80,000 people who consumed my creations and hired me to work with them. As Kelly predicted, a smaller percentage of these were 'True Fans', purchasing virtually everything I produced. I'd stumbled upon a universal 'value formula' that's used by companies who want to address new audiences and by church leaders who want to grow their congregations. Teachers use it to engage their students and teenagers use it to enlarge their social circles. *The Clarity Value Formula* has three elements: visibility, value and clarity.

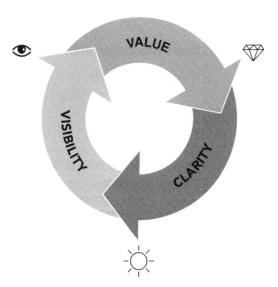

Figure 19.1:   The CLARITY® Value Formula

1. Clarity

Each of us is unique, with our own talents, abilities and perspectives on life. Clarity of understanding allows you to see through contaminated thinking and move boldly forward to make a difference with what you have.

2. Visibility

Value is exchanged in the context of relationships. If you want to create value for people, you need to become visible enough *to each other* for a relationship to be initiated.

3. Value

People don't pay for what *you* value; they pay for what *they* value. Whether they're paying with money, attention, time or energy; the more highly they value a result, the more they're willing to pay. So what's the value you want to create, and how does it deliver the results your audience is looking for?

Case Study: From time-based to results-based

John Wilkes was working full-time for a consultancy firm, but he told me about his dreams of working for himself, with the income and freedom to be truly independent (John loves the outdoors and wanted to spend less time working and more time fishing.) I started asking questions about John's boss (the owner of the consultancy). 'What results does your boss want? Why does he want those results? What problems keep him awake at night?' John realized he didn't know that much about what really mattered to his employer. I tasked him with finding out and, by the next week, John had made himself more *visible* to his boss and got clarity about what his boss *valued*.

John was working long days and saw that much of his time was spent doing things that didn't directly contribute to the results that mattered most to the company. I asked him, 'What could you achieve if you organized your time and energy at work to focus only on achieving the results your boss values?' By our next meeting, John had come up with a plan. If he eliminated all the superfluous activities, and focused only on results, he could deliver what his boss wanted at a much higher level than he was currently doing, while working only three days per week (although they would be *long* days).

Now came the challenging bit: John wanted to move from full-time to three days per week while keeping his *existing* salary! He was anxious about even *proposing* this to his boss, worrying it might damage their relationship, or even get him fired. As I helped him get clarity, John had an insight: he had a strong relationship with his boss, and realized that he would appreciate John being honest and transparent with him. While he still felt a little nervous on the day, he presented his proposal from a place of clarity, authenticity and connection. His boss accepted it, later revealing that *he'd* learned something valuable in the process: John's example underlined that what mattered to his business was *results*. His boss realized that if he could rely on them being achieved to a high standard, then it made sense to pay people for their *results* rather than their hours.

That was six years ago. John now runs a successful digital marketing agency, and has launched Hotfishin.co.uk, a website that connects fishermen with fisheries (imagine a kind of 'Airbnb for fishing'). He's taken his use of *The Clarity Value Formula* to a new level, becoming *visible* to fisherman and fisheries, and creating *value* for both audiences. His increasing grounding over the years has given him the courage, creativity and insight he needed to take action and play a bigger game. In the process, he's moved from selling his time to providing the results his audiences value.

CLARITY   plus   **ACTION**   equals   **RESULTS**

Figure 19.2:   The CLARITY® Results Model

Separate realities revisited

Remember: we each live in our own THOUGHT-generated perceptual reality. As you get clarity about who you want to become visible to, it can be profoundly useful to find out more about how *they* see the world. This can help you get clarity about three important things:

1 What they perceive as value.

2 How you can provide that value, or something they'll value even more highly.

3 How you can connect with, engage and educate them to the point where they're able to make an *informed decision* about what you're offering.

The better you understand your audience's world view (e.g. what they believe, value, fear, desire, struggle with etc), the more easily you can connect with them, and the more eloquently you can communicate with and educate them. (You'll find a downloadable PDF with a list of questions that can help you start to 'get' an audience's world view at the 'additional materials' weblink at the end of this chapter.)

Case Study: From searching to finding

At the beginning of 2013, author, coach and speaker Marina Pearson decided she wasn't going on any more courses. She'd been searching for years and had spent a lot, but she wasn't getting a return on that investment. Then Marina read my book *CLARITY* and something clicked. She joined one of my programmes, and her world started to transform. In the next six months, she. . .

- delivered a TED talk

- moved to Bali (one of her dream locations)

- became pregnant after trying for years with no luck

- started running workshops and filling them easily

- started signing up longer-term coaching clients for the first time, and enjoying the process.

Let's look at Marina's journey through the lens of *The Clarity Value Formula:*

- *Clarity:* While she had plenty of skills and information, Marina had been caught up in the outside-in misunderstanding. But as you start waking up to where your experience comes from, you start to see more clearly who you really are, and what you're capable of. This is what started happening for Marina.

- *Visibility:* As a result, she became more aware of the opportunities that were *already* there for the taking. We're surrounded by opportunities, but when we're caught up in contaminated thinking, we often overlook them or shrink from them. Marina started noticing opportunities, and saying 'yes' to them. And this resulted in. . .

- *Value:* Marina was able to share her unique gifts and abilities with the people who resonated with her. This led to some of those people wanting to have *more* of what she offered, so she started saying 'yes' to bigger opportunities, and taking on bigger challenges.

After years spent searching and struggling to make a living, Marina found the inner source of fulfilment and security, and had her best year yet (both experientially and financially). She said, 'I've finally been able to stop searching and start living the life of my dreams!'

Of course, when you take on bigger opportunities and challenges, it sometimes shines a light on areas where you're *not* seeing the inside-out nature of life, and it's time for another increase in your grounding. *The Clarity Value Formula* is a virtuous circle. As you grow in any one of the three areas, you're inspired to grow in the others.

Practicality check: How is *The Clarity Value Formula* going to help me get results?

If the results *you* want are in any way reliant on other people, *The Clarity Value Formula* will help you engage them in your efforts. Whether you're selling your ideas to your boss, your services to your clients or your values to your children, this formula can help you get clarity, engagement and results.

So once you know what journey you want to take people on, how do you influence people to come on the journey with you?

Bottom line results: Businesses have two basic functions which produce results: marketing and innovation. *The Clarity Value Formula* has three elements: Visibility (marketing), Value (innovation) and Clarity (being the person or organization who can deliver the value to the audience). As such, *The Clarity Value Formula* is a universal formula for business results.

keep exploring ❖ connect with others
share your discoveries ❖ deepen your understanding

Experiment: What are some of your ideas about how you can start becoming visible to certain audiences? What are some of the ways you can already start to imagine creating value for them?

www.jamiesmart.com/results19

20

Influence, Motivation and Zero-Pressure Persuasion

People are silently begging to be led.

Jay Abraham, Consultant, author

'Put up your hand if you don't like selling. . .'

Whenever I ask this question, the majority of the audience raise their hands. When I investigate, I inevitably discover that their experience of selling (or being sold to) involves some form of creepiness, manipulation or pressure. In a nutshell, they feel bad about it. But the process of influence is not only essential to enrolling other people in your initiatives; done effectively, it's also one of the most powerful ways there is for you to serve others. Whether you're selling your services to your clients, or your ideas to your colleagues. . . Whether you want to persuade an entire market to buy your product or your teenager to make a wise choice about their education. . . the ability to influence others is an essential skill for results-creators.

It's not about you

So why do people so often feel uncomfortable with the idea of sales, persuasion and influence? Because most of our models of persuasion and influence are of it being done *badly*. The word 'selling' conjures up out-of-date images of cheap-suited hucksters using high-pressure manipulation tactics. We recoil at the thought of having to trick, bully or cajole people into doing what we want them to do. But that's not what effective influence even *looks* like.

Influence isn't about getting what you *want by pressuring, cajoling or bullying. . .*
It's about helping people get what <u>they</u> *want through connection, education and collaboration.*

You see, people don't want what matters to *you*; they want what matters to *them*.

People don't pay for what you offer. . .
They pay for the transformations they desire. . .
The stories that reflect their values. . .
The results they want to create. . .
And the way they want to feel.

The payment can take many forms, including (but not limited to): money, attention, time, labour, expertise, barter, connections, endorsements, introductions, referrals and prestige. What people pay for can also take a variety of forms. . .

- While a dealer may be selling a car, the purchaser may be paying for safety (Volvo), speed (Bugatti), school-run status (Range Rover) or prestige (Lamborghini), as well as the narratives and feelings that accompany those experiences.

- While a supermarket may be sourcing organic vegetables, the shopper may be paying for their future health, a delicious meal, a feeling of vibrancy or the opportunity to tell themselves an authentic story (e.g. about caring for their family's health).

- While a software vendor may be selling a new package, the CTO he's selling to may be buying a feeling of security or the sense that they haven't made a bad decision (when I worked in the IT industry, people half-joked that 'nobody ever got fired for buying IBM').

- While a shoe manufacturer may be producing luxury footwear, their customers may be investing in their self-image; a story they're telling themselves about confidence or coquettishness, about seduction or style.

And this is the key: the only things anyone ever pays for are the transformations they desire, the results they want to create, the stories that reflect their values and the way they want to feel.

The secrets of ethically effective influence

In Chapter 9, you read about Pete Bryceland, the coach who struggled to enrol clients. When he was speaking with a potential client, he'd listen deeply to the person and start feeling connected to them. Pete would identify results that could justify the client enrolling with him, but when it came time to discuss them signing up, Pete started feeling uncomfortable and uneasy. Then the *client* started feeling uncomfortable and uneasy.

Unsurprisingly, when conversations went this way, they didn't result in Pete signing up a client, and he felt frustrated. When I talked it through with him, I told him he had good reason to be hopeful. I said, 'You already have everything you need to become a master of ethical influence; you've just had something getting in the way – contaminated thinking'. You see, your experience of the *influencer* is a major factor in whether or not you go ahead with a purchase.

Nobody likes being influenced by a person who. . .

- you feel uncomfortable with or pressured by

- you don't like, don't trust and don't feel connected to

- is a poor listener

- doesn't care about you or the relationship, and only has their own interests at heart

- doesn't know what they're talking about

- is unwilling or unable to take the lead, and wants you to do it for them

- is committed to you doing what's *right for them*.

Everyone likes being influenced by a person who. . .
- you enjoy interacting with

- you like, trust and feel connected to

- is a good listener

- cares about you, the relationship, and has your best interests at heart

- knows what they're talking about

- is willing to gently lead you in a direction you want to go

- is committed to helping you arrive at the decision that's *right for you.*

The number one influence factor

One of the biggest factors when it comes to buying something is the experience the client has of being influenced by you. If they have a great experience of you influencing them, they're much more likely to buy what you're selling.

So what's the biggest factor that determines whether or not a client will have a great experience of being influenced by you?

The experience *you're* having of influencing them. People pick up on 'where you're coming from'. If you're feeling needy, uncomfortable and manipulative, they're likely to feel creeped out, uncomfortable and manipulated. If you're feeling calm, connected and inspired, they're likely to feel calm, connected and inspired.

The secret of zero-pressure persuasion

When you truly listen to another person, you fall out of your insecure, self-centred thinking and fall into a feeling of connection with the person you're listening to. Connection carries its own credibility; as the feeling of connection emerges, your client's trust in you deepens, and they'll tell you more about what really matters to them. Listening and connection are the key to 'getting your client's world', and to discovering what's valuable and important to them. The experience of connection is like an 'influence accelerant' that telegraphs warmth, credibility and trustworthiness. It helps create a space where people can fall out of the La-la Land of their fears and anxieties, and fall into alignment with what really matters to them. This is the domain of education and collaboration. Nobody likes to feel pressured, wheedled or manipulated. Everybody likes to feel seen, respected and treated fairly.

Case Study: Recovering a client relationship

When we met, Juan Jose Quesada was working as an account executive for SAP. He experienced a profound transformation after participating in a weekend workshop with me, and booked a place on my coach training programme the following week. A week after that, he emailed my office saying he'd decided not to proceed with the programme. I was puzzled at his change of heart, so we scheduled a Skype call.

When Juan first appeared on-screen, his arms were crossed and he seemed abrupt and defensive. This was in stark contrast to the warm, connected experience we'd had last time we'd spoken. 'What do you want from me?' he asked. Unbeknownst to me, Juan had googled me and read that I was a 'master of influence'. He was afraid that he might be manipulated during our call, and had even written a note to himself warning him not to re-enrol on the programme. His anxiety and tension were obvious; he was caught up in contaminated thinking.

I explained that I'd enjoyed connecting with Juan, and that while I liked the idea of him coming on the programme, what I most *cared* about was our relationship. I assured Juan his money would be refunded within the next 24 hours, and said that the training pro-gramme was off the table for now; that I wouldn't even attempt to re-enrol him during this call. He began to relax, and the sense of connection started to re-emerge. We talked about the insights he'd had, his hopes and dreams and about what he planned to do next. By the end of our conversation, the earlier discomfort had evaporated and we were feeling the deep sense of connection we'd enjoyed previously. Our relationship was intact.

A week later, Juan reached out to say he'd had *another* change of heart. He'd been deeply impacted by our conversation and impressed by my commitment to the relationship. He said he defi-nitely wanted to go ahead with the programme. Since then, Juan has trained as a *Clarity Coach*, and is now working with entrepre-neurs and company directors in the Spanish market. In fact, he's now earning more as a coach than he was as an account executive.

Ask for what you want

A key element of sales, persuasion and influence is the call to action. Whether it's asking for the order or inviting someone on a date, you need to give people the opportunity to take the next step. I'm mentioning this obvious point because, while it may *sound* like common sense, it's astonishing how often contaminated thinking (masquerading as fear of rejection) obscures it.

A key point: every aspect of what you do with your client is part of the client experience: your marketing, your sales process, your delivery, your referral process, your follow-up. All of it. The more pristine your client's experience is when they're with you, the more smoothly everything goes in your client relationships.

Practicality check: How is influence, motivation and zero-pressure persuasion going to help me get results?

The ability to influence is one of the keys to creating results that involve others. But many people struggle to be influential in the very places where it's most important. If your result involves other people, you need to be an influencer.

So once you've influenced someone to come on the journey with you, and you have an idea about how you can deliver their dream result, how do you turn your idea into a reality?

Bottom line results: In business, your influence amplifies your impact. The art of influence starts with finding out what matters to the other person. People don't want what *you* want; they want what *they* want; the transformations they desire, the stories that reflect their values, the results they want to create, and the way they want to feel.

---

keep exploring ∴ connect with others
share your discoveries ∴ deepen your understanding

Experiment: What are the people in your audience already on the lookout for? If you can determine what your audience perceives as valuable, important and desirable, it becomes much easier to present what you offer in a way that is attractive, relevant and compelling to them.

www.jamiesmart.com/results20

21

Turning Ideas into Reality

....

The future cannot be predicted, but futures can be invented.

Dennis Gabor, Physicist, engineer, winner of the Nobel Prize in Physics, 1971

'The goal is to eradicate chronic psychological suffering globally for everyone by 2030. . .'

I felt overwhelmed by the churn of emotions: worry, excitement, anxiety, inspiration. For many years, I'd been exploring and sharing the principles behind clarity. I'd also been describing my vision of a generation of children being born into a world where the adults already understand the pre-existing fact of the 100% inside-out nature of life.

But all this time, I'd had a secret: while I passionately believed in my vision, and was committed to doing whatever I could to help bring it into being, I'd been afraid to put a deadline on it. The vision already seemed so enormous, so overwhelming, so full of uncertainty. . . Setting a goal, creating a project and going public with a deadline seemed too big – like an invitation to fail. So I'd been playing it safe; stopping short of what I was inspired to create. And that's when I had a realization. . .

Your feelings aren't telling you about the risk of failure,
the size of the goal or your ability to achieve it. . .
Your feelings are an experience of the principle of
THOUGHT taking form right now, in this moment.

The area where I was feeling *the most* inspired was also the area where my contaminated thinking had seemed most real. The moment I realized this I knew, 'You have to take action and move forward with your goal.'

The goal is to eradicate chronic psychological suffering
globally by 2030.

New passion and energy came flooding in. As I started to tell people about the goal, it started taking on a life of its own, and I learned something anew that every great results-creator intuitively understands.

The creative process is at the heart of how you turn ideas into reality.

Many people are confused about how to make things happen, and get stuck making excuses and giving up on their dreams. But when you understand the creative process, you can use it to overcome obstacles and create results that seem extraordinary or even impossible.

There's no such thing as a creative person

There's no such thing as a creative person; there are merely people who have learned how to dance with the creative energy of life. The fact that you can see, hear or feel – the fact that you're having an experience right now – means that you're connected to MIND; the creative energy of life. It's creating your experience right now, in this very moment.

Who are some of the creators you admire?

Stop for a moment and think about some of the creators or creations you admire. Here are some of my favourites to spark your imagination:

- Frank Zappa (composer of numerous awesome pieces of music)
- Barbara Marx Hubbard (visionary futurist)

- Antoni Gaudí (ground-breaking architect)

- Lynne Twist (global visionary and fund-raiser)

- Jimmy White (the most inventive snooker player ever to hold a cue)

- Adam Curtis (extraordinary documentary maker)

- Jane McGonigal (game designer and pioneer)

- Daniel Kitson (greatest storyteller I've ever heard)

- Quentin Tarantino (incredible film director)

- You (co-creator of the life you're living)

These people are *co-creators*. They danced with the creative energy of life to bring those creations into being. You are far more creative than you realize. And just as you've danced with this creative energy to create the life you're living, you can dance with life to create the results you desire.

It starts with an idea

The creative process begins with an idea, often an authentic desire (something you want just because you want it). The idea often arrives as an insight or realization. It doesn't have to be 'realistic'; its job is to point you in a direction. Remember: your authentic desires are an expression of the infinite intelligence and creative potential that we're all part of; the formless principles of THOUGHT, CONSCIOUSNESS and MIND.

How to deal with resistance

Authentic desires are sometimes followed by feelings of insecurity (aka 'resistance'). Flavours include, 'I don't know how', 'I'm not enough' and 'What if I fail?'

IMPLICATION: Your conception of the future is not reality; <u>now</u> is reality

'Resistance' is an expression of the outside-in misunderstanding; feelings that are letting you know about THOUGHT taking form in the moment, and nothing else. I was working with a client who was feeling very stuck. I asked them if they believed the 'stuck' feelings were telling them about (a) their future situation, (b) THOUGHT in the moment or (c) a mixture of their thinking and the future situation. As I suspected, they chose (c). While most people are willing to accept that their thinking's got *something* to do with their felt experience, they believe that the future situation (for instance) has got at least *something* to do with it too. But that's not real. 100% of your state of mind is an experience of THOUGHT in the present moment. The future does not yet exist, so none of your felt experience can be coming from the future.

	Solar system	Germ theory	Human experience
A.	A. Sun goes round earth	A. Bad smells cause infection	A. Feelings are letting you know about the future
B.	B. Earth goes round sun	B. Germs cause infection	B. Feelings are letting you know about THOUGHT in the moment and nothing else
C.	C. They take turns	C. A bit of both	C. Feelings are letting you know about a mixture of the future and THOUGHT in the moment

Developing your creative process

Novelist E.L. Doctorow said, 'Writing is like driving at night in the **fog**. You can only see as far as your headlights, but you can make the whole trip that way.' I heard this when I was starting a business in January 2003. I loved what he was pointing to, and used this idea as the basis for how I developed the company. You see, there are three powerful things implied by this simple quote:

1 *Destination:* you have a 'good enough' sense of the destination you're heading for. You may not know exactly how to get there, and you may not be clear on every single detail of what your destination looks, sounds and feels like, but

there's something you know for sure: you have a sense of your destination that's 'good enough' that once you get there, you'll know you've arrived. This mean you're already in a position to begin. You don't need to know what every mile of the journey will look like in detail.

2 *Power:* you have a power source and a means of moving forward. In the case of the car, this includes the engine, driveshaft and wheels, as well as the fuel in your tank. In the case of your life and the results you want to create, the power source is your innate capacities and instincts (the *deep drivers* we explored in Chapters 1 and 6). The fact that you can sense the destination means there's a way for you to move forward.

3 *Navigation:* the combination of your headlights, the instruments on your dashboard and your controls allow you to respond to the ever-changing environment and make adjustments where necessary. Similarly, when you set out to create results, your senses, memories and embodied understanding allow you to use expertise, intuition and sensory data to sense the terrain and respond accordingly.

Remember: you're built for reality. You're capable of so much more than you think you are, and you're better than you realize at responding in the moment. We're all connected to this 'inner guidance system' capable of helping us navigate. When we're caught up in contaminated thinking, we believe we need to 'solve' the resistance before we can move forward, but that's not true. You're capable of more than you think, because you *are* more than you think. As you start moving forward, you will be guided.

How you turn ideas into reality

(1) Take the next step. (2) Calibrate. (3) Repeat. . . As you step out of La-la Land and move forward in the reality you're built for, the path will emerge before you.

CLARITY   plus   **ACTION**   equals   **RESULTS**

Figure 21.1:   The CLARITY® Results Model

Practicality check: How will developing my creative process help me get results?

You're a born results-creator. Contaminated thinking is the most common obstacle to creating results. As you move forward in spite of 'resistance', you'll discover your own 'flavour' of creation.

In May 2016, the UK Charities Commission approved our application to establish *The Clarity Foundation*, with the following purpose:

> *The Clarity Foundation's purpose is to relieve chronic psychological suffering globally.*

The only way we can tackle such an enormous result is using the creative process; using our 'good enough' sense of the destination to guide us in taking the next step, seeing and taking the opportunities that present themselves along the way.

So how do you amplify your results to impact the world on a massive scale?

Bottom line results: Innovation is at the heart of business, and is the only sensible response to the rapidly changing business landscape of the twenty-first century. Whether you're a one-man band or leading an enterprise with many thousands of employees, every person in your organization is connected to the creative intelligence of life. The more you're able to utilize the creative intelligence that already exists within your company, the more likely you are to prosper in this rapidly changing environment.

keep exploring ❖ connect with others
share your discoveries ❖ deepen your understanding

Experiment: At the end of Chapter 7, I invited you to reflect on some of the results you'd love to create. Now I'd like to invite you to get into action. Choose a result. Do you have a 'good enough' sense of your destination that you'll know it once you get there? What's the very next step you could take towards making it into a reality?

www.jamiesmart.com/results21

22

Leveraging Your Results Exponentially

Any company designed for success in the 20th century is doomed to failure in the 21st.

David S. Rose, Author, angel investor, Inc. 500 CEO

'I hate timelines. . . deadlines. . . basically I hate all lines. . . I just want to make all the things. . . all the time. . .'

Amanda Palmer's Patreon.com video shows the kimono-clad songwriter using hand-lettered signs to make a request while music from her 2012 album, *Theatre is Evil*, plays in the background. The album was released following a 31-day Kickstarter campaign that raised $1.2 million, but her new video was announcing a much bolder venture. Patreon's MTP is 'to help every creator in the world achieve a sustainable income'. The platform allows creators to secure pledges from members of their tribes and then collects those pledges on an agreed basis (per month, per song, per work of art etc). The request Palmer makes is simple; she's asking for help. She explains that she wants to make things, and that whether she gets 100 pledges or 10,000, she's going to 'make all the things'. Early in her career, Palmer earned her crust as the Eight Foot Bride, a living statue who offered a flower and a moment of connection to the passers-by who put money in the hat at her feet. Today, she continues to innovate, building connection and impact with her audience. Patreon has effectively automated 'the hat', allowing her to get enormous leverage.

Most of us have been conditioned to exchange our time for money, with salaries, day rates and 'charge by the hour' models. But one implication of the commercial transformation can mean transcending this Industrial Revolution model and discovering new ways to generate value and income. Fortunately, it's never been easier. Digital technology is rapidly transforming the ways we can get leverage. Social technologies have given all of us the kind of communication power historically reserved for governments and only the largest organizations. We all have the tools – now what are you going to do with them? How are you going to use these opportunities to create value?

The rise of the machines

Economist and mathematician Eric Weinstein suggests that the logical extension of the information revolution is this: everything we do based on *human expertise* will eventually be replaced by a computer. The leverage point for value is to move away from 'expertise' and towards a model based on the cultivation of connection, creativity and insight. Once again. . .

We have to recognize and harness the power of exponential insight if we want to sense and respond to the challenges of the digital age.
We have to understand the nature of THOUGHT if we are to survive and thrive as individuals, as organizations, as societies and as a species.

The impact of exponential technology is going to be unimaginably large. For instance. . .

- According to *Fortune* magazine, a billion women will be joining the global economy by 2020 as entrepreneurs or employees, and will dramatically alter the world of business.

- At least three billion additional people (mostly from Africa, India and China) are due to come online by 2020, with high-speed internet and smartphones.

- Current predictions suggest that there will be over 10 million autonomous cars on the roads by 2020.

- There are already sensors in billions of objects (cars, TVs, lights) connecting them to the internet. That's predicted to grow to trillions by 2030.

- The resulting wearable technology will mean we're able to take more control of our own healthcare, diagnosing illness quickly and accurately.

- Robots are already being tested in areas where they can go far beyond human limits in terms of precision and accuracy (e.g. eye surgery).

- Opportunities to leverage community and crowd will only increase, as people become more connected.

These powerful drivers are changing the nature of work and how we think about it. So how do you stay relevant in a VUCA world?

Staying relevant in a VUCA world

The Institute for the Future (IFTF) produced their *Future Work Skills 2020* report in 2011 to look at the key skills, abilities and competencies that the workforce of 2020 is going to need in response to the trends referred to above. They updated it in 2016 to include 'Resilience' (in light of our need to adapt in the face of the increasing speed of change). All of these 'future-skills' depend on your ability to draw on your *deep drivers*; the innate capacities you were born with. Here's the IFTF list:

IFTF Future Work Skills 2020	Brief definition	Deep drivers/ innate capacities these rely on
Resilience	The ability to competently overcome setbacks, challenges, and other obstacles.	Resilience, Creativity
Sense-making	The ability to perceive the deeper meaning of situations, and have the insights and realizations necessary for decision making.	Clarity, Creativity, Intuition, Presence
Social intelligence	The ability to be emotionally fluent and connect deeply with others to build strong relationships and collaboration.	Connection, Presence, Authenticity, Intuition
Novel and adaptive thinking	The ability to come up with unique and relevant solutions in unexpected situations.	Clarity, Creativity, Intuition
Cross-cultural competency	The ability to adapt quickly and operate in a variety of contexts and cultures, and as a member of diverse teams.	Connection, Resilience, Presence
Computa-tional thinking	The ability to make decisions based on large data sets, but also to act in the absence of key data.	Intuition, Presence, Clarity
New media literacy	The ability to produce and 'read' video and other new media as fluently as people now produce and read text.	Resilience, Creativity, Intuition

IFTF Future Work Skills 2020	Brief definition	Deep drivers/ innate capacities these rely on
Transdisciplinarity	Literacy in and understanding of multiple fields, in order to solve problems that require multi-disciplinary solutions. This requires curiosity and the willingness to keep learning.	Presence, Resilience, Clarity
Design mindset	Organizing your approach, environment and thinking to support different kinds of tasks and outcomes.	Presence, Creativity, Direction
Cognitive load management	The ability to deal with the increasing barrage of information, being strategically selective about what is and isn't given attention.	Clarity, Resilience
Virtual collaboration	The ability to be productive, engage others and (potentially) to lead others as part of a virtual team.	Presence, Connection, Clarity, Direction

In a world where new technologies, platforms and engagement models are emerging every month, the illusion that we can look to the external world to provide a sense of security and stability is no longer viable. That sense of security and stability can *only* come from within. As you deepen your understanding of subtractive psychology, and your sense of inner security continues to increase, you'll find yourself experiencing more and more freedom to experiment.

Practicality check: How is exponential leverage going to help me get results?

The technologies you need to exponentially leverage your results *already exist*, and new ones are being created every day. You have the ability to learn about them, use them and experiment with them. In fact, the only thing that *ever* stops people from learning and experimenting is contaminated thinking, showing up as fear: fear of failure, fear of criticism, fear of the unknown, fear of change, fear of loss etc. You live in a world of opportunity. Exponential results come from insight, experimentation and action.

Every experiment is an opportunity for learning. And while they may not always turn out the way you expect them to, experiments <u>always</u> get results.

| CLARITY | plus | ACTION | equals | RESULTS |

Figure 22.1: The CLARITY® Results Model

At the time of writing (January 2018), Amanda Palmer's Patreon channel showed 11,084 patrons pledging to pay $38,247 for each 'thing' she produces (an average of $3.45 per patron per thing). She inspires a loyalty in her audience that is based on authenticity, transparency and genuine connection.

So how do you create the kind of transformational experiences your audience desires?

Bottom line results: The world of work is changing rapidly. With new ways of working come the need for new skills and qualities. As the demand for these skills continues to increase, the prizes will go to the individuals and organizations who manage to leverage their innate capacities and instincts. Creativity, perceptiveness and social intelligence underpin the work skills that are going to be essential in 2020 and beyond.

keep exploring ⁖ connect with others
share your discoveries ⁖ deepen your understanding

Experiment: An experiment is something you create in order to test an idea, so what's an idea you'd like to test? What's an experiment you can perform to test that idea? Design it, test it and learn from your results.

www.jamiesmart.com/results22

23

The Key to Creating Transformational Experiences

Long experience has taught me that the crux of my fortunes is whether I can radiate good will toward my audience. There is only one way to do it and that is to feel it. You can fool the eyes and minds of the audience, but you cannot fool their hearts.

Howard Thurston, Magician

'Do you want to know the biggest leverage point for improving the quality of your customers' experience?'

I was having an initial meeting with the general manager of a luxury hotel, and the subject of TripAdvisor ratings had come up. The site's user-generated reviews have a big influence on the hospitality industry, and one of his objectives was to get the hotel into the top 10 for his city. He told me about the obstacles he was up against: high turnover among millennials, increasingly demanding customers, changes in buying habits driven by new technology. He talked about the results he wanted to achieve: a stronger brand, higher engagement and productivity, attracting, retaining and developing the best talent. When I asked him my question, he looked slightly amused and invited me to tell him. 'The biggest leverage point for improving the quality of your customers' experience is the quality of the experience you and your team are having.' He looked shocked, and said he agreed. He told me that he passionately believed this, but that I was one of the only people he'd ever met who held the same view. I asked him what he'd tried, and he told me about a variety of efforts to build a stronger, happier team. Some had worked well, while others had not. Some people had been impacted, while others were unaffected. I said I understood, and asked, 'Do you want to know the single biggest influence on the quality of you and your team's experience?' He did.

Your understanding of how your experience is created is the ultimate leverage point for improving the quality of that experience.
The more deeply you understand the principles behind clarity, the more you benefit from your mind's ability to self-correct to resilience, creativity and connection.

Expectations are increasing – high-quality products and services are the minimum requirement, and people want them now. So how do you create the kind of transformational experiences that lead to great reviews, valuable referrals and raving fans? It turns out that the most powerful leverage point for impactful customer experiences is *inside the mind of the customer*. The only place value can *ever* be created is in the mind of the audience. Value is in the mind of the beholder, and is an emergent property of the relationship. And where all the elements of value come together is in the customer experience.

The fish rots from the head down

Remember the *Harvard Business Review* article showing that leaders' states of mind are 'transmitted' to other people? This is not a new observation; an ancient proverb captures the infectious nature of contaminated thinking in the phrase, 'the fish rots from the head down'. But it turns out that the same infectious quality is true of the calm, happy, energized states that drive high performance, connection and positive experiences. Companies that are renowned for the quality of their *customers'* experiences (e.g. Apple, Southwest Airlines, Zappos) recognize the fact that it's correlated to their *employees'* experiences.

So what exactly is the culture of a company, a community or a society?

The Employee Experience Drives the Customer Experience

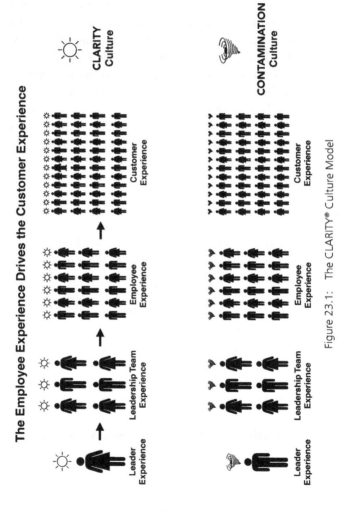

Figure 23.1: The CLARITY® Culture Model

Culture is the expression of a group's level of consciousness; their collective clarity of understanding. And the thoughts, words, actions and artefacts that make sense from that level of understanding.

While there will be various *expressions* of that level of under-standing, the thing that *drives* them is the level of conscious-ness behind them. As an organization's collective clarity of understanding increases, things that used to be normal stop making sense, and things that used to seem impossible are sud-denly sensible and straightforward.

The day-to-day expression of a group's level of understanding determines the collective state of mind it operates from. This affects numerous important factors, all of which correlate to the deep drivers we've been exploring (e.g. purpose, direction, resilience, agility, experimentation, insight, creativity, innova-tion, problem solving, connection, community and the 'feel' of the brand). Here's a simple way of thinking about it. . .

Contamination days: You know those days when it probably would have been better if you'd stayed under the duvet. . . When nothing seems to turn out right, and it's almost as if you're working against yourself. . . And it's stressful and unproduc-tive. . . And everything seems like a struggle and a chore. . . And you finish the day wondering where it went, with nothing to show for it but a headache and more on your to-do list.

Clarity days: And then there are those other days when you can't seem to put a foot wrong, and everything's falling into place. . . Those days when it's almost as if you're being guided, and you're unusually productive. . . Feeling at ease, yet focused. . . Coming up with great ideas, and finding solutions easily. . . And you finish the day with a sense of accomplishment, feeling fulfilled and satisfied with a job well done.

The kind of day a person is having determines whether they're showing up as a plus or a minus in their organization. And while most of us have both of these kinds of days from time to time, their frequency and duration is a function of your clarity of understanding. As you get a deeper understanding of subtractive psychology, you'll find yourself having fewer 'contamination days' and more 'clarity days'. Perhaps best of all, the self-correcting nature of the mind means that even if you start out having a bad day, it can turn into a clarity day in a heartbeat, because. . .

The thing that transforms your experience from contamination to clarity is a realization. . . an insight. . . a fresh new thought.
And you're <u>wired</u> for insight, because you're built for reality. . . Optimized for success, with the factory settings for creating results.

The deeper your understanding of the principles behind clarity, the more easily you'll find yourself defaulting to the factory settings.

Reality check

'Are you saying that if everyone in my company is in a good mood, then our customers will be too? That seems like cloud cuckoo land!' I'm not saying that. Your clients and customers are paying for the results that matter to them. But their *experience* is going to depend on more than just the results they get or the transformation they go through; it's also going to be a function of the way they *feel*. As we head towards a trillion-sensor world, and see virtual technologies being used to create blended realities (where the digital world is blended with the physical world), companies will have more and more influence over the external and internal aspects of a person's experience. But, as I wrote in my first book, *CLARITY...*

> *The value of an event is dependent on the quality of the experience the person has. The quality of the experience a person has is 100% dependent on their level of clarity when they're having the experience. This is why understanding the nature of THOUGHT is so fundamental to the experience economy.*

Of course customers are paying for the results that matter to them. High-quality products and services are now expected as standard. But here's the thing: you can go to the best restaurant in the world. It doesn't matter how good the restaurant is, how good the service is or how good the food is; if you don't have a great *experience*, it's likely to get a one out of five on TripAdvisor.

By the same token, you can go to a restaurant that *isn't* so great; where the food is so-so, or the service leaves something to be desired. But if you have a great *experience*, chances are you're going to give it a good rating. Remember:

Your customer's feelings are giving them feedback about the 'glasses' they're wearing, not who or what they're looking at. Their experience will be consistent with their level of clarity in the moment.

The customer's experience always comes from THOUGHT in the moment. If they're in a bad state of mind, they'll tend to blame it on the restaurant, the food or the people they're with. No matter how good the service, they'll find something to take issue with. No matter how exquisite the meal, it won't be up to scratch. Conversely, if they're in a good state of mind, then they're likely to attribute it to the food, the restaurant and the people they're with. If they're in a good feeling, they'll be more likely to overlook or forgive poor service, bland food or drab decor.

Of course, if the service, food and decor are first-class *and* your customers are in a good feeling, you're on track for a five-star review.

How to turn a one-star circumstance into a five-star experience

So what's going to have the biggest influence on the 'glasses' your customers are wearing? The 'glasses' *you and your employees* are wearing. Moods are infectious, but clarity of understanding is a powerful inoculator. As you deepen your understanding of the inside-out nature of life, you'll be less likely to 'catch' the negative moods of your colleagues and customers, and be more capable of leading them in a positive direction. And here's the thing: mistakes may still happen from time to time, but your ability to respond from a place of resilience, connection and clarity is the thing most likely to turn a situation around, and put a smile on a customer's face. That's how you turn a one-star circumstance into a five-star experience.

Practicality check: How are transformational experiences going to help me get results?

These days, high-quality products and services are expected; your biggest leverage point is your clients' *experience* of what you offer. The most powerful way to influence that is through the experience you and your team are having. And the most powerful way to influence *that* is your understanding of the principles behind clarity.

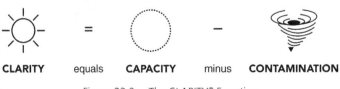

| **CLARITY** | equals | **CAPACITY** | minus | **CONTAMINATION** |

Figure 23.2: The CLARITY® Equation

So now that you know the key to transformational experiences, how do you prosper in the transformation economy?

Bottom line results: Companies that are renowned for the quality of their *customers'* experiences recognize that they're correlated to the quality of their *employees'* experiences. The kind of day a person is having determines whether they're showing up as a plus or a minus in your organization. The kinds of days the people in your organization have are an expression of the *clarity of understanding* of those people. Another word for this is 'culture'. If you want to increase the number of 'plus' days in your organization, your biggest leverage point is an increase in clarity of understanding.

---

keep exploring ⁙ connect with others
share your discoveries ⁙ deepen your understanding

Experiment: Start looking out for the link between state of mind and the quality of experience a person is having. Before long, you should start to notice a strong correlation between the two.

www.jamiesmart.com/results23

24

Prospering in the Transformation Economy

....

A new type of thinking is essential if mankind is to survive and move toward higher levels.

Albert Einstein, Physicist, winner of the Nobel Prize in Physics, 1921

'Really, the only thing that makes sense is to strive for greater collective enlightenment. . .'

Elon Musk's statement shocked me. Greater collective enlightenment? Musk is one of the founders of PayPal; the creator of Tesla Motors, SpaceX and Solar City. He was the inspiration for the screen persona of Tony Stark, the whisky-swilling, billionaire playboy engineer-turned-superhero in the *Iron Man* films. Then suddenly, it all fell into place. . . Musk's *purpose* is the evolution of human consciousness. He's using technology, insight and action to succeed where governments and legacy industries are failing. His companies attract top talent; purpose-driven high performers exhilarated by the chance to make a difference in the world. The factories rely on advanced robotics to build automobiles, space vehicles and solar power cells. The fleet of Tesla cars is a 'learning network', leveraging sensors, wireless connectivity and artificial intelligence to collect and make sense of vast amounts of data. With every mile travelled, the fleet gets smarter, and the domain of driverless cars gets closer.

The exponential nature of technology is transforming our world at an ever-increasing pace. Robots are becoming more versatile and artificial intelligence is becoming more commonplace. As computing power continues to get faster and cheaper, whole categories of employment will disappear. The jobs at the highest risk of automation are those involving repetitive tasks and expertise that can be specified and codified. The jobs at the lowest risk of automation are those requiring high degrees of perceptiveness, creativity and social intelligence. There's an obvious conclusion you can draw from this. . .

The capacities you need to prosper in the twenty-first century can be summarized as perceptiveness, creativity and social intelligence.

The data shown in Figure 24.1 have been 'cherry-picked' from a list of over 700 jobs spread across the range from low

Probability that jobs will be eliminated as a result of innovations in digital technology (including computerization, robotics and artificial intelligence)

(0 = low vulnerability to computerization, 1 = high vulnerability to computerization)

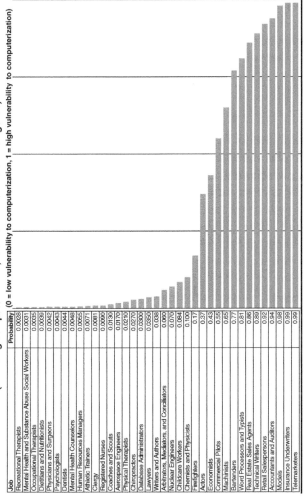

Job	Probability
Recreational Therapists	0.0028
Mental Health and Substance Abuse Social Workers	0.0031
Occupational Therapists	0.0035
Dietitians and Nutritionists	0.0039
Physicians and Surgeons	0.0042
Psychologists	0.0043
Dentists	0.0044
Mental Health Counselors	0.0048
Human Resources Managers	0.0055
Athletic Trainers	0.0071
Clergy	0.0081
Registered Nurses	0.0090
Coaches and Scouts	0.0130
Aerospace Engineers	0.0170
Physical Therapists	0.0210
Chiropractors	0.0270
Database Administrators	0.0300
Lawyers	0.0350
Writers and Authors	0.038
Arbitrators, Mediators, and Conciliators	0.060
Nuclear Engineers	0.070
Childcare Workers	0.084
Chemists and Physicists	0.100
Firefighters	0.17
Actors	0.37
Economists	0.43
Commercial Pilots	0.55
Machinists	0.65
Bartenders	0.77
Word Processors and Typists	0.81
Real Estate Sales Agents	0.86
Technical Writers	0.89
Retail Salespersons	0.92
Accountants and Auditors	0.94
Models	0.98
Insurance Underwriters	0.99
Telemarketers	0.99

Source: THE FUTURE OF EMPLOYMENT: HOW SUSCEPTIBLE ARE JOBS TO COMPUTERISATION? by Carl Benedikt Frey and Michael A. Osborne, 2013

Figure 24.1: Susceptibility of Jobs to Exponential Technologies

probability of computerization to high probability. This has been done (a) for reasons of brevity and (b) to shine a light on the extremes, highlighting the jobs with the lowest and highest risk of automation.

The rise of the transformation professional

A large number of the jobs at an extremely *low* risk of automation involve *transformation professionals* (e.g. psychologists, clergy, physicians, nutritionists, coaches); roles where much of the value is created through connection, creativity and insight. The growth of the 'wellbeing industry' has seen hundreds of thousands of people drawn to the 'profession of transformation'. As our global consciousness continues to rise, industries are disrupted and working patterns change, with people seeking greater independence and freedom. We're being drawn to values-based, purpose-driven work that utilizes our gifts and passions. And when it comes to perceptiveness, creativity and social intelligence. . .

You're already connected to the source of creativity and innovation.
You're already optimized to thrive as a socially intelligent being.
You're already endowed with the powers of perceptiveness and persuasion.

These capacities are as integral to your nature as your ability to see, hear or feel. The only thing that slows your development or gets in the way is contaminated thinking arising from the outside-in misunderstanding. The reason people have struggled to teach these 'emotional intelligences' until now is because they've been trying to do it using *additive* approaches. But remember: embodied understanding is *subtractive*. As your understanding of subtractive psychology continues to increase, your capacities for creativity, perceptiveness and social intelligence automatically come to the fore.

CLARITY   equals   **CAPACITY**   minus   **CONTAMINATION**

Figure 24.2:   The CLARITY® Equation

Clarity of understanding gives rise to the qualities you need to thrive, prosper and create meaningful results in the twenty-first century. As you get a deeper understanding of the principles behind clarity, you automatically benefit from your innate capacities, and increase your bandwidth and selectivity for learning the skills and capabilities that *aren't* innate. Your ability to create results relies both on your innate capacities, and on the skills and abilities they enable you to learn.

Case Study: What would you do if it was OK to fail?

Christina is passionate about nutrition, but by day she was working as an auditor. She was getting enquiries from people wanting to work with her, but she'd been hit by a paralysing mix of emotions. She suddenly doubted her ability to do the work she loved, and was gripped by 'fraud' feelings, asking: 'Who am I to do this?' Her parents wanted her to stick with something 'safe', like her current job. Christina was terrified at the thought of failure, and of disappointing her parents, so she asked me for help. In the midst of our conversation, I asked a standard 'coaching question'. . .

Jamie: What would you do if you couldn't fail?
Christina: I'd do it. I'd become a nutritionist.
Jamie: Great. Here's a slightly different question. What would you do if it was OK to fail?
Christina: Same thing. I'd become a nutritionist.
Jamie: Great. That means the only issue you've <u>actually</u> had is that you didn't realize that it's <u>OK</u> to fail.

Failure is a concept; it doesn't exist in *reality*. Every time you do an experiment, you get a result. It may not be the result you *wanted*, but you can learn from it and feed that learning into the next experiment. I said, 'You weren't born with a fear of failure, otherwise you would never have learned to walk or talk.' And like learning to walk and talk, success in a new enterprise is built on a foundation of numerous experiments. That's part of the nature of learning.

Christina said she understood, but still felt worried at the thought of making a mistake and disappointing her parents. After exploring this with her for a few minutes, I said. . .

> *You're feeling THOUGHT in this moment, not the future*
> *or other people's opinions.*
> *Your feelings are giving you feedback on the glasses you're*
> *wearing, not what you're thinking about.*

We looked up 'nutritionist' on Frey and Osborne's chart (see Figure 24.1) and found they'd evaluated it as among the *least* likely of all jobs to be computerized. According to their research, being a dietician or a nutritionist is one of the safest jobs there is. We then looked up Christina's current job role, 'auditor'. Frey and Osborne scored it among the *most* likely of all jobs to be computerized.

Christina realized that the jobs her parents considered *safest* were actually among the *most* vulnerable. The job that looked the most *dangerous* to them was actually one of the *least* vulnerable.

Christina's passion for nutrition, combined with her willingness to experiment with social media, mean that she's well-placed to prosper in the transformation economy. When I followed up with her recently, she'd decided to 'give it her all', and is now working as a nutritionist. She said, 'What I do every morning is wake up with a smile on my face; I love my life, I love what I do every single day.'

Closing the gap

The philosopher Gregory Bateson wisely pointed out that 'The major problems in the world are the result of the difference between how nature works and the way people think.'

You can view the evolution of human knowledge and understanding as a process of closing the gap between how reality <u>already works</u> and the way we <u>believe</u> it works.

The closing of that gap is a reflection of the increase in our collective level of consciousness; humanity's clarity of understanding. And as humanity's level of consciousness continues to rise, we see the external expressions of that evolution. . .

• The infant mortality rate has declined dramatically over the past 100 years.

• Rates of murder and other violence continue to fall; we live at the most peaceful time in human history.

• Billions of people are able to communicate with each other.

• The number of countries adopting democratic systems continues to increase.

• Tolerance and acceptance of alternative lifestyles is on the rise.

- People are demanding greater transparency, authenticity and integrity from businesses.

- Companies are scrabbling to bring more 'emotional intelligence' into the workplace.

- More and more people are inspired to do values-based, purpose-driven work.

The move towards greater independence, freedom and purpose is an expression of this increase in humanity's clarity of understanding.

Remember, for practical purposes, you have the ability to perceive yourself as distinct and separate from the rest of life. But you are never *actually* separate. You are inseparable from the intelligence and oneness of life, part of an undivided whole. I invite you to open to the possibility that the reason so many people are seeking values-based, purpose-driven work is because our collective consciousness is continuing to rise.

We live at a pivotal point in history. While in many ways things are better than ever, we also face some of the biggest threats yet to our existence as a species, including climate change, artificial intelligence, radical fundamentalism and poverty. In September 2015, the United Nations announced a set of 17 Sustainable Development Goals (SDGs) with the aim of massively transforming the quality of life for *all* life on the planet.

Here is a summarized version of the SDGs:

- End poverty everywhere
- End hunger and improve nutrition
- Ensure good health and wellbeing
- Ensure quality education for all
- Achieve gender equality
- Clean water and sanitation for all
- Affordable and clean energy for all
- Decent work and economic growth
- Industry, innovation and infrastructure
- Reduce inequality
- Safe, sustainable cities and settlements
- Sustainable production and consumption
- Combat climate change
- Conserve oceans and marine resources
- Protect and sustain life on land
- Peace, justice and strong institutions
- Partnerships for achieving these goals

The SDGs represent massively transformational results for the whole of humanity. A quick analysis will reveal that the achievement of these goals will be the result of the level of consciousness of the people involved in them, and the actions that level of consciousness inspires.

Our collective clarity of understanding is the ultimate leverage point for creating results in our own lives, and for all of humanity.

Transforming negative VUCA to positive VUCA

Futurist and former president of the IFTF, Bob Johansen, suggests that there's a counterpoint to the often overwhelming 'negative VUCA' of volatility, uncertainty, complexity and ambiguity; the 'positive VUCA' of vision, understanding, clarity and agility. And what transforms negative VUCA into positive VUCA?

Foresight. . . Insight. . . Realization. . .

The IFTF creates scenarios to give leaders 'foresight'; a 'feel' for possible futures. As leaders reflect on these future scenarios, they often have insights and realizations relating both to the present, and to the way forward. In the face of insight, volatility inspires vision, uncertainty resolves to understanding, ambiguity gives way to agility and complexity yields to clarity.

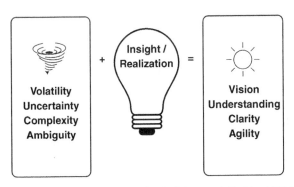

Figure 24.3:   Negative VUCA plus Insight equals Positive VUCA

Practicality check: How is understanding the transformation economy going to help me get results?

We're right at the start of the most disruptive phase in human history; the challenges we face are significant. As Einstein said, if mankind is to survive and move towards higher levels, it will come as a result of actions born from a *new* type of thinking; an increase in our individual and collective consciousness.

| CLARITY | plus | ACTION | equals | RESULTS |

Figure 24.4: The CLARITY® Results Model

We're all on this journey together, hurtling through space at 67,000 miles per hour. The fact that you're reading this book means that you're already increasing your understanding of subtractive psychology and the principles behind clarity. As you get a deeper embodied understanding of how the mind already works, *who you really are* will be showing up more and more of the time. This is the path to the kind of results worth creating, and the kind of success worth having.

Bottom line results: Perceptiveness, creativity and social intelligence are key to business prosperity in the next 20 years. People already have these capacities; the only thing that slows development or gets in the way is contaminated thinking. Remember: embodied understanding is subtractive. As your understanding of the principles behind clarity continues to increase, your capacities for creativity, perceptiveness and social intelligence automatically come to the fore.

keep exploring ⁘ connect with others
share your discoveries ⁘ deepen your understanding

Experiment: At the beginning of this book, I asked you a question: What's the number one result that – if you were to achieve it – you believe would have the biggest positive impact in your life? Ask yourself this question again, or get someone else to ask you. It can be fun to compare your answer now to the answer you gave when you first started this book. What are some of the things you're inspired to do, create or become, moving forward?

www.jamiesmart.com/results24

Acknowledgements

....

My heartfelt thanks and appreciation go to. . .

All my teachers, colleagues and clients, past and present.

The pioneering community of Clarity coaches, consultants, trainers and practitioners who are with me on this adventure.

The people who have so generously allowed me to tell their stories in this book: Ani, Ankush, Christina, Donna, Ian, Jim, Jo, John, Juan, Katherine, Mahima, Mamoon, Marina, Pete, Tallulah, Tilly and the Council of the Institute and Faculty of Actuaries.

Patrick Cumiskey, for introducing me to the fighter within.

Dean Jackson, for more cheese and less whiskers.

Tom Oxford Smith, for your collaboration, patience and beautiful artwork.

The team at Capstone, for your support and expertise.

Robin Charbit and Ken Manning, PhD, for your wisdom, simplicity and encouragement.

Michael Neill, for your friendship, your insight into my direction and for patiently pointing me towards these principles.

Dicken Bettinger, Keith Blevens PhD, Cathy Casey, Chip Chipman, Mark Howard PhD, Rita Shuford, Cheryl Bond and Jan Chipman and for your friendship, guidance and mentorship on the Clarity programmes.

Chantal Burns, for your love, fun and invaluable feedback.

Garret Kramer, for your friendship and wise counsel.

Keith Blevens and Valda Monroe, for your friendship, the single paradigm and everything else.

Chip and Jan Chipman, for your friendship and for speaking directly to who I really am.

Shaa Wasmund, for your friendship, mentorship and for asking me the number one result question all those years ago.

Deborah Banner, Jonny Bowden, Jacob Collins, Steven Heath, Dawn Hines, Emma McDevitt and Dzidek Sabat for your passion, genius and tireless support.

Nikki Owen, for your love, and for keeping the wheels on for all this time.

Tilly, Boo and all my family, my heart is filled with gratitude and love for you.

And finally, to Sydney Banks, for uncovering the principles behind clarity and sharing them with the world.

Further Explorations

These are the books I most frequently recommend to (and often purchase for) my clients, friends and family. . .

The Missing Link by Sydney Banks (Lone Pine Publishing, 1998)

Instant Motivation: The Surprising Truth Behind What Really Drives Top Performance by Chantal Burns (Pearson, 2014)

The Path of No Resistance: Why Overcoming Is Simpler Than You Think by Garret Kramer (Greenleaf Book Group, 2015)

Stillpower: Excellence with Ease in Sports and Life by Garret Kramer (Simon & Schuster, 2012)

Invisible Power: Insight Principles at Work by Ken Manning, Robin Charbit and Sandra Krot (Insight Principles, 2015)

The Inside-Out Revolution: The Only Thing You Need to Know to Change Your Life Forever by Michael Neill (Hay House, 2013)

The Space Within: Finding Your Way Back Home by Michael Neill (Hay House, 2016)

CLARITY: Clear Mind, Better Performance, Bigger Results by Jamie Smart (Wiley, 2013)

The Little Book of Clarity by Jamie Smart (Wiley, 2015)

RESULTS: Think Less, Achieve More by Jamie Smart (Wiley, 2016)

You can find more educational materials, including audios, videos and distance learning programmes at. . .

www.JamieSmart.com

CLARITY® for Transformation Professionals

....

Jamie Smart is passionate about supporting transformation professionals (E.g. coaches, trainers, consultants, therapists, change-workers etc.) in bringing the principles behind clarity into their work with clients, into their own practices and into their lives.

If you're passionate about making a difference, Jamie has a variety of programmes serving the growing community of transformation professionals who are leveraging the principles behind clarity in their work with clients and growing their practices. These include virtual courses, 1:1 coaching and the *Clarity Certification Programmes*.

All the programmes are oriented around the three essential transformations you need to share this understanding at a professional level: 1) *Grounding* – deepening your embodied understanding of these principles, 2) *Impact* – increasing your ability to share this understanding with others and

3) *Leverage* – discovering the keys to making your living 'from the inside-out' and taking your practice or business to the next level. These programmes are also popular with entrepreneurs, business owners and other leaders who want to bring an understanding of these principles into their work and their lives.

If you're a transformation professional and want to take things to a new level, here's what to do next:

1   Download the book **The Thriving Coaches Scorecard** to identify your sticking points, leverage points and quick wins for taking your grounding, impact and practice to a new level. It's a quick read with a powerful effect, and you can get it for free at *www.JamieSmart.com/scorecard*

2   Join the **Thriving Coaches Group** on Facebook and connect with the growing community of like-minded transformation professionals who are passionate about exponentially increasing their grounding, impact and their livelihood. You can join for free at *www.JamieSmart.com/thriving*

3   Subscribe to the *Thriving Coaches Podcast* for free at *www.JamieSmart.com/TCP*

You can find details of the *Clarity Certification Programmes* at. . .

www.JamieSmart.com/professional

CLARITY® for Personal Results

Do you want to experience greater clarity and more meaningful results in specific aspects of your life? Experience shows that as you get a deeper understanding of the principles behind clarity, you'll start noticing the *inevitable results* of living more closely in alignment with the reality you're built for. Some of the results people typically experience include. . .

– An effortlessly clear mind more of the time, with less stress and more clarity

– Better relationships, with more love and connection

– Healthier choices and improved decision-making

– Greater sense of purpose and courage, with less struggle and strain

– An increased ability to create the results that matter to you and for you

Here's what to do next:

1 Discover your personal *CLARITY® Quotient* by answering 20 simple questions (multiple-choice). This quick and easy

questionnaire gives you a snapshot of your current state of mind, including a stress score and an engagement score. You can get yours for free at *www.ResultsBook.org/CQ*

2 Subscribe to the podcast, *Get Clarity with Jamie Smart* for free at *www.JamieSmart.com/ClarityNow*

3 Get free access to the *Clarity Results Community,* a Facebook group where you can connect with like-minded people as we support each other in creating the results that matter to you and for you at *www.JamieSmart.com/ClarityResults*

www.ResultsBook.org/challenge

CLARITY® for Business

Jamie Smart and his team work with a variety of businesses ranging from an SME ranked as one of *The Sunday Times 100 Best Small Companies to Work For* to a Fortune 500 business designated by Ethisphere as one of the *World's Most Ethical Companies*. Jamie Smart has keynoted conferences for organizations ranging from *Hewlett Packard* to the *Council of the Institute and Faculty of Actuaries*. Some of the services we offer include:

– Keynote speeches on topics including:

  o Mental clarity

  o Cultivating a results mindset

  o Leadership in a rapidly changing world

  o Resilience in times of uncertainty

  o Coaching for performance and results

– Executive coaching and 1:1 intensives

– Teambuilding workshops and leadership retreats

– Consulting projects to solve specific business issues

To find out if your organization is a good fit for a Clarity project, get in touch with us on *business@jamiesmart.com*

Subtractive Psychology

"Subtractive psychology" is a term coined by Jamie Smart to refer to the radical new approach to resilience, wellbeing and mental health described in this book. It is being used with dramatic results (under a variety of names by leading-edge practitioners) in domains as diverse as elite sports, blue-chip companies, treatment centres, business start-ups and even the penal system.

The power of subtractive psychology lies in its simplicity: The field is grounded in the discovery (by the philosopher Sydney Banks) that there are principles that govern human psychology, just as there are fundamental principles that govern the natural world. As an individual develops an embodied understanding of the principles behind clarity, they start to 'see through' conditioned psychological habits such as stress, worry and anxiety.

This understanding is (as the name suggests) entirely subtractive, taking things off people's minds and allowing their innate capacities to come to the fore. As a person has less on their mind, their innate resilience, wellbeing and peace of mind shine through more fully and effortlessly allowing them the freedom to experience life to the full, flourish and thrive.

www.SubtractivePsychology.com

The Clarity Foundation

....

The *Clarity Foundation* is a not-for-profit social enterprise created with the aim of relieving chronic psychological suffering globally. Our vision is for children to be born into a world where people have a foundational understanding that clarity is the mind's natural state and that innate psychological wellbeing exists within all of us. The *Foundation* provides programmes, coaching, training and education based on the principles behind clarity.

To find out more and to see how you can get involved, please email info@worldclarity.com or visit

www.WorldClarity.com

About Jamie Smart

Jamie Smart is a Sunday Times bestselling author, speaker and executive coach who presents regularly at major conferences world-wide. He shows individuals and organizations the unexpected keys to clarity; the ultimate leverage point for creating profound transformation and meaningful results.

Jamie's primary focus is in showing transformation professionals and business leaders how to bring the principles behind clarity into their work with clients, into their own businesses and into every aspect of their lives. In addition, he works with a handful of 1:1 coaching clients and leads selected corporate programmes.

Jamie has keynoted conferences for organizations ranging from *Hewlett Packard* to the *Council of the Institute and Faculty of Actuaries*. His corporate clients range from a Fortune 500 business designated by Ethisphere as one of the *World's Most Ethical Companies* to an SME ranked as one of *The Sunday Times 100 Best Small Companies to Work For* to. He has appeared on Sky TV and on the BBC, as well as in numerous publications including *The Times, The Daily Telegraph, The Huffington Post* and *Psychologies Magazine*. As well as *The Little Book of Results,* he is also the author of the books *RESULTS: Think Less, Achieve More, CLARITY: Clear Mind, Better Performance, Bigger Results* and *The Little Book of Clarity*.

Jamie lives in the UK. When he's not working, he loves spending time with his daughters, travelling, walking, drinking coffee and exploring.

You can read Jamie's blog and find his podcasts at www.JamieSmart.com or wherever you get your podcasts.

You can also connect with him on the following social media sites:

Instagram:	@JamieSmartCom
Twitter:	@JamieSmartCom
Snapchat:	@JamieSmartCom
Facebook:	www.Facebook.com/jamiesmartcom
YouTube:	www.youtube.com/jamiesmartcom
LinkedIn:	https://www.linkedin.com/in/ JamieSmartClarity

You can find full contact details at:

www.JamieSmart.com

Printed and bound by CPI Group (UK) Ltd, Croydon, CR0 4YY

25/03/2025

14647324-0001